THE
DICE GAME OF
SHIVA

Also by Richard Smoley

Conscious Love: Insights from Mystical Christianity

Forbidden Faith: The Secret History of Gnosticism

The Essential Nostradamus

Inner Christianity: A Guide to the Esoteric Tradition

Hidden Wisdom: A Guide to the Western Inner Traditions
(with Jay Kinney)

First Flowering: The Best of the Harvard Advocate, *1866–1976*
(editor)

Praise for Richard Smoley's *The Dice Game of Shiva*

"*The Dice Game of Shiva* takes a legendary account of creation and demonstrates its usefulness in the twenty-first century. This beautifully written book draws material from several disciplines, weaving a seamless fabric that is both original and practical, both timeless and contemporary. There are many 'theories of everything' in today's bookstores, but many readers will find Richard Smoley's tour de force the most intriguing and the most persuasive."
— Stanley Krippner, PhD, professor of psychology at Saybrook University and coauthor of *Extraordinary Dreams*

"*The Dice Game of Shiva* carries the reader insightfully through metaphor, a breadth of references, and insight into the diaphanous realms of consciousness. Richard Smoley's fascinating examples and challenging thinking invite readers to explore meaning and applicability to their own spiritual journeys. Exploration of the relationship between consciousness and its experience plays throughout the text and draws the reader to a deeper experience of self. I recommend this text for any student of mind and purpose."
— Betty Bland, president of the Theosophical Society in America

"This is an exciting, powerful book on the nature of mind and its relation to the universe. It is hard to put down. It is written largely from an Eastern viewpoint by a man who has, here and elsewhere, demonstrated his comprehensive knowledge of the Western searchings. (See, for example, his book *Hidden Wisdom*.) The depth and extent of Hindu psychology and philosophy of mind is little known in the West. This book has been long needed. One cannot read it without emerging feeling somehow 'more,' an inner stirring and movement in new directions, the same sort of feeling you have when you see *Guernica* for the first time or really hear the *Appassionata*. Do not pick it up unless you are prepared for this."

— Lawrence LeShan, PhD, author of
A New Science of the Paranormal and *How to Meditate*

"I have a standing rule: I read anything Richard Smoley writes — and *The Dice Game of Shiva* proves once again that I'm correct to do so. This book is a profoundly wise examination of the nature of consciousness and its place — *our* place — in the universe. Smoley's writing is engaging, personal, and elegant. Anyone interested in the origin, nature, and destiny of consciousness should read this important book."

— Larry Dossey, MD, author of
The Power of Premonitions and *Healing Words*

"I loved Richard Smoley's *The Dice Game of Shiva*, which thoughtfully deals with conundrums from consciousness to causality. He quotes the Indian dharma master Ramana Maharshi, who teaches the nondual view that it is impossible to be separate from an infinite God, or infinite consciousness. He similarly describes the inseparability of consciousness from the contents of consciousness — thereby dismantling the so-called mind-body problem. And he convincingly attacks the illusion of causality with which we try to order our lives, quoting Bertrand Russell, who wrote that causality 'is a relic of a bygone age . . . like the monarchy.' "

— Russell Targ, physicist and author of *Limitless Mind*

THE
DICE GAME OF
SHIVA

HOW CONSCIOUSNESS
CREATES THE UNIVERSE

RICHARD SMOLEY

New World Library
Novato, California

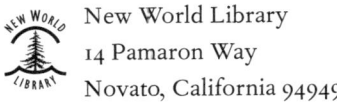

New World Library
14 Pamaron Way
Novato, California 94949

The permissions acknowledgments on page 201 are an extension of the copyright page.

Text design by Tona Pearce Myers

Library of Congress Cataloging-in-Publication Data
Smoley, Richard.
  The dice game of Shiva : how consciousness creates the universe / Richard Smoley.
    p.   cm.
Includes bibliographical references and index.
ISBN 978-1-57731-644-2 (pbk. : alk. paper)
  1. Religion—Philosophy. 2. Consciousness. 3. Experience. I. Title.
BL51.S5885 2009
210—dc22   2009033391

First printing, November 2009
ISBN 978-1-57731-644-2
Printed in the United States on 30% postconsumer-waste recycled paper

New World Library is a proud member of the Green Press Initiative.

10 9 8 7 6 5 4 3 2 1

For Robert Krier Smoley

CONTENTS

ACKNOWLEDGMENTS

First I would like to thank my dear wife, Nicole, and my little son, Robert (to whom this book is dedicated), for providing me with a loving home in which this book could be created.

In addition, I appreciate the help and support of my agent, Giles Anderson, and my editor, Jason Gardner, for enabling me to shape my ideas into a finished book. Thanks are also due to Kristen Cashman and Bonita Hurd for their careful attention to the manuscript in the editing process.

Finally, I am grateful to Joy Mills and Gerald J. Larson for their thoughtful reading of the manuscript and for helping me to sharpen my insights. Of course any errors and omissions in this book remain my responsibility and not theirs.

Richard Smoley
Winfield, Illinois
March 2009

A KABBALIST AT OXFORD

The threads of most books can be traced to any number of points in their authors' lives. If I were to place the genesis of this book somewhere in particular, I would choose the late 1970s, when for two years I was a student at the University of Oxford.

I admit that I had no well-defined reason for going there. I had received a bachelor's degree in classics from Harvard, and, having my mind set on a literary career, I vaguely thought it would be useful to polish off my Greek and Latin studies with a degree from Oxford in Literae Humaniores ("more humane letters"), also known as Greats, a celebrated course in which one studied ancient history, classical literature, and/or philosophy. Each student had to choose two of the three; I chose the latter two.

The picture of Oxford that many Americans have is an idyllic one, and the school is usually imagined as it might have been around 1910, with the men in straw boaters and the women in Edwardian gowns. In this world, viewed through a soft focus, the principal occupations are tea parties, cricket, flirtations, aristocratic whimsies, and adolescent despair. There one occasionally drops in on one of the dons and engages in witty repartee over glasses of brown sherry, or falls in love with the daughter of an earl, only to be spurned because of one's social inferiority.

All this had little to do with the actualities of 1978. While there were glimpses of this past (to the extent that it was ever real), the dominant mood was much less frivolous. At least it was so in my college, Corpus Christi — Oxford is divided into colleges, each with its own history, atmosphere, and traditions. Corpus was tiny, with some two hundred undergraduates, but it had an august scholarly reputation, particularly in the classics. Over time I would learn that this reputation rested not so much on genius as on an extraordinarily well-honed pedantry. In one of Robertson Davies's novels (I don't remember which), one of the characters has his genealogy traced by an owlish and desiccated Corpus man. This was the spirit of the place, and while many students did not fit the mold — the graduate students, with whom I tended to socialize, were, fortunately, a more diverse and worldly lot — there were many who did.

I was not among them. I was a restless and dissatisfied student, constantly grumbling and frequently depressed. Although I'd enjoyed the Greek and Latin classics as presented in the more relaxed world of Harvard, I found the prescribed course in Greats curiously dull. The menu in literature, for example, included the *Thesmophoriazusai,* one of Aristophanes' less funny comedies, in which the tragedian Euripides sneaks into the women's rites for Demeter; the later elegies of Sextus Propertius, written when this intense and refined poet had carved himself into a literary monument; and the second half of *The Aeneid*, a section so tiresome that it may explain why Vergil wanted to have the poem burned after his death.

But it was philosophy that truly baffled me. I do remember moments of triumph — a funereal December afternoon when I rose from a battered oak table in the reading room of the Bodleian Library and congratulated myself on finally having read the entirety of Plato's *Republic* in Greek, and the following spring, when I set myself to read Aristotle's *Nicomachean Ethics*, again in the original, over the course of a single week, largely because I wanted to take the spring holiday off for a trip to Egypt. It was good that I did, because in Egypt I fell ill with a form of dysentery that somehow transformed itself into a severe shoulder infection, forcing me to miss most of the next term.

The masterpieces of Plato and Aristotle, though not always compelling reading, are deservedly renowned, and as texts they formed a superb introduction to philosophy. The method of instruction at Oxford was, however, somewhat peculiar, at least to someone used to American education. There were no courses in the sense familiar to us. Your entire degree depended on ten or eleven essay-style examinations, which you took at the end of your time there. The dons did not grade you in the meantime, although you were called before a panel at the end of every term and told how well or poorly they expected you to do. There were any number of lectures, but these were not required and were generally underattended. The heart of the program was a weekly meeting with a tutor, who supplied you with a reading list that you were to use as the basis of an essay. You read the essay aloud the next week, and then the tutor made his or her comments.

At its best this type of instruction no doubt promotes a sharp and subtle interaction that hones the minds of both pupil and teacher. I did not encounter it at its best. My chief tutor in philosophy was a balding, bespectacled man with strange mannerisms that included hunching over his armchair and scratching the carpet with his fingers in a manner that seemed oddly simian. His taste in attire (say, a wide-lapelled jacket of some unrecognizable material, matched with a pale purple shirt and an interestingly striped tie) led one of my friends to remark, "He dresses like his wife buys his clothes." I will never forget the time when, while reading an essay aloud, I mentioned as an example of an incorrect belief the idea that World War II began in 1941. He must have been only half-listening, because he looked up sharply and said, "For some of us it began a bit before that!" "I said it was an *incorrect* belief," I replied. "Oh," he grunted and went back to scratching the carpet.

I studied with him for a year and a half, and never for a single second did I have the impression he was anything but utterly bored with me and my intellectual productions. How could it have been otherwise? He had heard the same essays on Plato's cave and Aristotle's concept of virtue over and over again, for years upon years; it was extremely unlikely that I — or anyone else who was neither transcendentally brilliant nor frankly insane — could have come up with something he had not heard before.

The rest of the philosophy curriculum was equally peculiar. If you had not known otherwise, you could have easily concluded that, with the exception of a few stray insights from Descartes and Hume and Kant, nothing of the slightest interest had occurred in the field between the death of Aristotle in 322 BC and the rise of logical positivism in the 1930s. It was only midway through my time there that I realized what was really going on. I was not surveying the discipline of philosophy in any broad sense; I was attending a particular school of philosophy. It was Oxford philosophy, with its own heritage and trends and dogmas, and one could no more expect complete impartiality there than one could have expected it at the school of Pythagoras or the Academy of Plato.

Thinking for oneself was ostensibly encouraged, but the

correct line was clear. Religion was generally regarded with a tolerant, though occasionally irate, bemusement. Certainly there were religious believers at Oxford, as well as a chapel in every college; there were even "permanent private halls" with names like Blackfriars and Greyfriars that were intended for training clergy, but these seemed remote and obscure. (An issue of *Oxford Today* magazine informs me that Greyfriars, founded by the Franciscan order, closed its doors in June 2008.) Among philosophers, it was tacitly acknowledged that one would be an atheist or agnostic. In moral philosophy, utilitarianism was the right view, and some even took it to the point of embracing the then-novel cause of animal rights. Metaphysics was avoided: examining such issues as being and existence was the sort of thing they did on the Continent, along with eating snails and driving on the wrong side of the road. Philosophy of mind was a trickier matter. The simplistic equation of the mind with the brain — a view known as materialism — presented too many philosophical problems to be entirely accepted, but nothing more plausible had taken its place. The prevailing view was a vague functionalism holding that the mind arises out of the functioning of the brain, although how this happened was never entirely explained or understood (as it still isn't).

All in all, it was a philosophy of "nothing but." God is nothing but a crutch for the weak; the mind is nothing but the brain or the operations of the brain; morality is nothing but the maximization of pleasure and the minimization of pain for the greatest number (possibly including beasts). Indeed "nothing but" ranks, along with the common law, industrial manufacture, the men's suit, and Stilton cheese, as one of the major contributions of the British people to world civilization. Although it was transmitted to the United States along with a language and a tradition of hopeless ineptitude at cooking, Americans, with their bizarre and incoherent longings for transcendence, have never been quite successful at replicating the smug assurance with which the British can pull off this attitude of "nothing but."

I did not take well to it. My own more mystical nature rebelled, and in any case I could see the enormous number of holes in the accepted views. Animal rightists could (and sometimes did) argue that a full-grown cow has more of a right to life than a newborn human baby. The philosophy of mind was a blank space to be filled in: philosophers seemed to be waiting like Vladimir and Estragon for a scientific vindication of materialism that they were sure would come any day now. What was most bewildering, however, was that every now and then one would see a particular conclusion dismissed as "counterintuitive." I could not help asking what exactly this intuition was that served as a touchstone for the most intricately reasoned arguments, and, if it was so reliable, why we did not drop the arguments and trust our intuitions to begin with.

It did not take me long to grow demoralized by this course of study. My last trimester there, the spring — or as it is called, Trinity — term of 1980, was taken up with review for the final exams that I would sit for in June. I found the philosophy review classes so worthless that soon I simply stopped attending, and I decided that I was going to have to figure it all out on my own. My strategy worked successfully enough; at any rate my tutors were surprised at how well I did.

And yet to paint my two years at Oxford as uniformly dark would be an exaggeration. The social life, which for me was centered on the Middle Common Room — the college's watering hole for graduate students — was far more agreeable: talking till two or three in the morning with whoever happened to turn up, fueling the discussion with bottle after bottle of Jubilee, a superb brown ale created by an Oxfordshire brewery to commemorate Elizabeth II's twenty-fifth year on the throne; instruction in the game of go by Billy Swan, an affable and soft-spoken Scotsman with a doctorate in philosophy; a surprise birthday party thrown for me by my girlfriend, Antoinette, at which for the first and only time in my life I chain-smoked a pack of Dunhills; and the special dinners, held on Wednesdays every month or so, for which the college kitchen would cook a more elaborate meal than usual, and which partakers would accompany with wine bought from the buttery.

Despite these fond memories, and despite a certain intellectual rigor that the course of study imparted to me through all my resistance, my two years at Oxford would have seemed a total waste of time to me had it not been for an unforeseen circumstance that befell me soon after I arrived.

Thinking it would be fun to take part in some extracurricular activities, in my first week I went to the Freshers' Fair, a showcase for the various clubs and societies that flourished at the university. There were groups that put out publications with names like *Isis* and *Tributary* and *Vague*; there was the Lucky Jim Society, dedicated to "cycling aimlessly around the countryside"; there were the people who rode to hounds; and there were the people who harassed the people who rode to hounds. As I meandered among the representatives of these organizations, I came across a man with long hair, a scraggly beard, and a pair of very thick eyeglasses. He was, I would later learn, not a student but an employee at the Inland Revenue, Britain's equivalent of the IRS. He thrust a leaflet into my hand and said (anomalously, since it was October), "There you are, and a happy Christmas to you."

The flyer was for something called the Oxford Kabbalah Group. I knew what the Kabbalah was — in my last year at Harvard, I had begun to frequent the Mystic Eye, an occult bookshop (now long vanished) that was nestled in a basement on the edge of

Harvard Square — but I had never met anyone who knew anything about this tradition. In 1978, it had not yet attracted the attention of power-crazed urbanites or scholars desperate for untapped
fields of research. So I began going to the group's meetings, which
were held in the garret office of a junior fellow at Magdalen College.

You walked up to the top floor of one of the college's venera-
ble buildings, empty and half-lit in the evening, and went to a
medium-sized room under the eaves. There, on a mantel over a
fireplace containing one of those British electric fires that never
produce heat that can be felt more than three feet away, was a slab
of white Formica about the size of a small tabletop, onto which the
Kabbalistic Tree of Life was incised. A pair of candles stood on
either side of it, and a bottle of red wine warmed near the electric
fire, to be consumed with bread and cheese when the meeting was
done. There were never more than seven to ten participants, usually fewer, and the majority were not students at all but local people: Dave, the Inland Revenue employee; Ally, a member of the
grounds crew at Trinity College; a psychiatrist whose name I've
forgotten; Christine, a flirtatious thirtyish divorcée; Peter, our host,
a research fellow at Magdalen who was also the leader of the
group; and assorted others who came and went. None of us, or
practically none, were Jewish.

I continued to go faithfully for the whole two years I was there.
The week I came down with my shoulder infection was unfortunately the one in which I had taken the kitty (a small cloth purse
that held the group's financial resources, usually amounting to
seven or eight pounds) in order to buy bread and cheese and wine
for the meeting. I was far too sick to sit through it, but somehow
I managed to drag myself to Oxford Covered Market to pick up
what was needed. Weak with fever, I showed up at the group,
dropped off the food, and staggered back to my room.

I could never quite tell what my friends at Corpus made of it all. The group met on Wednesday evenings, so on weeks when there was a special dinner they were always puzzled to see me rush off afterward to this odd society that I belonged to. They seemed to consider it an amusing eccentricity of mine — not a bad thing in a place that is, after all, the world capital of amusing eccentricities. But to tell the truth, I was somewhat ashamed of my interest, knowing how far it was from the dominant intellectual climate. When people asked me about it, I usually put them off.

No one in the group knew a great deal about the subject, really. We had read a few books, and every term, Warren, one of the Kabbalists who had started the group, would come up from London and give us an informal lecture. One time we piled into Dave's car — a three-wheeled motorcycle painted the color the French call *caca d'oie* — and went to London to visit Glyn, the other founder of the group, who could always be found in the kitchen at the end of his long, narrow flat in Maida Vale, drinking endless cups of coffee or tea and smoking cigarettes that he rolled himself. I visited Glyn many times after that, up to the time of his death in early 2007; I found it unthinkable to go to the United Kingdom without seeing him and went more than once for that purpose alone.

None of this added up to the England I expected from reading the plays of Shaw or the novels of Evelyn Waugh, and every time I think about a part of the world I've never visited, I have to imagine that, like England, it bears only the most tenuous resemblance to the clichés about it. In retrospect I can see the unlikely circumstances of my spiritual initiation as a test of my ability to see past appearances. When the spiritual teacher G. I. Gurdjieff first met the aristocratic composer Thomas de Hartmann in 1915, he arranged a rendezvous at a seedy café in Petrograd populated with whores. De Hartmann was even more taken aback by the dirty cuffs on

Gurdjieff's shirt. And yet there was something in de Hartmann that enabled him to look past the facade; eventually he became one of Gurdjieff's most dedicated and important pupils. My own test was, unlike de Hartmann's, not deliberately contrived, but it made its own share of demands on me.

In the end, what led me to pursue Kabbalah and esotericism instead of hewing to the rigidities of Oxford philosophy was (apart from a deep-seated rebelliousness in my character) a sense of the dimensions of each. When we met in the Kabbalah group, our discussions were not always profound, and in fact were seasoned with a large dose of the silliness that could only be expected of beginners, but I had the sense of being surrounded by something greater — an unseen cosmos that was as infinite and mysterious as the night sky. When I turned to the ideas propounded in the dark-blue volumes published by Oxford University Press or in scholarly journals such as *Mind* and the *Philosophical Review*, I felt like a child who has been locked indoors on a summer day.

The skeptic — and today there is always a skeptic, inside us as well as outside us, one who haunts us as the devil haunted medieval monks — would say that this was a decision based on emotion rather than on reason. No doubt; but does that invalidate it? In recent years we have been introduced to the concept of emotional intelligence — an awareness and sensitivity to the felt nature of reality that is different from, and complementary to, intellectual intelligence. Why should our philosophy lack emotional intelligence, as it so often seems to do?

So it went. The Kabbalah group was shifting and mutable. People came and left, including Peter, whose office we had been using, so at the end of my second year we began meeting in the hopelessly shabby flat Antoinette and I shared on Walton Street in Jericho — a working-class district of Oxford that, disguised under the name "Beersheba," appears as the neighborhood of Jude the Obscure in Hardy's novel. Antoinette, whose father was an agnostic and whose mother was a diehard atheist, did not entirely approve of the group. She would usually arrange to be out on the evenings the meetings were held, and if she arrived home before everyone had left she would go upstairs to the bedroom and read.

A year or so after I came back to the United States, the group fell apart for reasons that were never explained, except by someone who obscurely remarked that "Christine turned it into a sex party." In a way I regret missing out on all the fun.

The story does not end there, of course. Over the years I kept in sporadic contact with people I had met through the group (there were similar ones meeting in London, Manchester, and Cambridge in those years), and today I'm still in touch with them through email and my regrettably infrequent trips to England. Warren Kenton, one of the group's founders, now lectures on the Kabbalah worldwide; his many books, published under his Hebrew name, Z'ev ben Shimon Halevi, are among the best and most authoritative treatments of the subject. As for me, I moved to San Francisco with Antoinette after we returned to the United States (we split up, amicably, a couple of years later), and for many years I struggled to reconcile what I had learned in England with what I experienced in the waves of New Age spirituality cresting in California in the 1980s.

To tell any more of my story would be to stray farther into the realm of memoir than I intend. I talk about it at such length because I can't help feeling that our civilization faces what I faced at Oxford: a choice between an arid materialistic philosophy that nonetheless remains academically prestigious and esoteric teachings that are profound and inspiring but often despised or ignored by the academic mainstream. At the time I did not have the intellectual apparatus to reconcile the two. Had I known more, I could have seen echoes of Plato's teaching in the Kabbalah. (Some in antiquity went so far as to claim that Plato learned everything he knew from Moses, although it's more likely that much of late Platonism eventually found its way into Kabbalistic thought.) What Plato called *doxa*, for example — usually translated as "belief" — corresponds almost exactly to the Kabbalistic Hod, often, though somewhat misleadingly, translated as "glory." (Significantly, *doxa* also sometimes means "glory," as in the last line of the Lord's Prayer.) The concepts of *doxa* and Hod both point to the level of consciousness that judges by appearances and externalities. What Plato called *noesis* — the perception of true reality in the eternal and unchanging Forms — the Kabbalah knows as Binah, or Understanding. I did not realize these things until much later, and it's just as well I didn't: discoursing on the Kabbalistic Tree of Life would not have sat well with the Oxford examiners.

This narrative may make it seem as if I'm about to proffer the Kabbalah as an instant solution to the intellectual and spiritual conundrums of our age. I am not. Although the Kabbalah remains the center point of my own spiritual path, and although many of the ideas I discuss in this book have Kabbalistic correlates, it so happens that the language of the Kabbalah doesn't always offer the most meaningful or accurate way of expressing them, and I've had to look farther afield. Moreover, the years between my time at Oxford and the present led me to explore many different paths: *A Course in Miracles*, Tibetan Buddhism, and Gurdjieff's teachings, among others, not to mention my eight years spent as editor of *Gnosis*, a now-defunct journal of the Western esoteric traditions. Each tradition has its own profound lessons to impart, and each casts a unique light on a transcendent reality that is ultimately beyond expression.

In recent years, it's seemed useful to formulate some of my ideas in the language of esoteric Christianity, if only because Christianity remains the religious core of our civilization. My books *Inner Christianity* and *Conscious Love* in particular are the results of this effort. Still more recently, I've found that certain Hindu schools of philosophy — particularly the one known as the Samkhya, which happens to be the oldest — speak in terms that correspond to my own train of thought. They address in a peculiarly powerful way the central issue not only of human life but also, perhaps, of all existence: the relationship between consciousness and the contents of its own experience — between *purusha* and *prakriti*, to use the language of the Samkhya, or between "I" and the world, to use the language of inner Christianity. I believe that this perspective presents some strong and possibly conclusive answers to questions that have vexed Western philosophy and religion since their origins.

CHAPTER ONE

THE LIGHT THAT GOVERNS
THE UNIVERSE

Languishing in a Nazi jail in June 1944, the theologian Dietrich Bonhoeffer wrote a remarkable letter to his friend Eberhard Bethge.[1] It is a haunting document, not only because Bonhoeffer would never live to flesh out his ideas (he would be hanged by his captors in April 1945), but also because, more than sixty years later, religion has not managed to solve — or frequently even face — the problem he sketched out. He writes, "Man has learnt to deal with himself in all questions of importance without recourse to the 'working hypothesis' called 'God.' In questions of science, art, and ethics this has become an understood thing at which one now hardly dares tilt. But for the last hundred years or so it has also become increasingly true of religious questions; it is becoming evident that everything gets along without 'God.'"

Humanity, Bonhoeffer goes on to say, has come of age. We don't need the idea of God to explain the workings of the universe; we are increasingly able to understand these things without it. Bonhoeffer's remarks echo the famous anecdote about the scientist

Pierre-Simon Laplace, who, at the turn of the nineteenth century, published a work containing calculations of planetary motions. Napoléon called him in for an interview. The emperor, who was fond of asking embarrassing questions, said, "Monsieur Laplace, they tell me you have written this large book on the system of the universe, and have never even mentioned its Creator." Laplace replied, "I had no need of that hypothesis." Napoléon, greatly amused, told the story to the mathematician Joseph-Louis Lagrange, who commented, "Ah! It is a beautiful hypothesis; it explains many things."[2]

Two hundred years later, we have, it would seem, still less need of "that hypothesis" than did Laplace. Science has closed up more and more of the causal gaps that divinities once had to fill. Unlike the ancients, we do not have to posit a hand of God that keeps the planets in their courses. Nor do we need a God to explain the origins of the cosmos or, very likely, of life. If there is an intelligence responsible for the universe, it is not the craftsman offered by conventional religion. Can we, then, jettison the idea of God, or, with Lagrange, shall we keep it not for its explanatory force but for its beauty?

Merely posing such a question will look like arrogance to the believer. Who are we to say we can take or leave the supreme ruler of the universe? It is not for us to decide such things; it is blasphemous to contemplate them. In any event, we have other needs for the idea of God. In 1788 Immanuel Kant wrote, "Two things fill the mind with ever new and increasing admiration and awe, the more often and steadily we reflect upon them: the starry heavens above me and the moral law within me."[3] Even if we have no more need of God to account for the starry heavens, don't we still require his services as the guarantor of the moral law within?

Not necessarily. An article in the British newsmagazine *The Economist* discusses how human beings differ from chimpanzees in their approach to fairness.[4] Scientists tested this by means of the ultimatum game, in which there are two players, a proposer and a responder. They have to divide a quantity of some good (which could be anything from cash to chocolates). The proposer chooses how much will go to him and how much to the responder. The responder has no choice but to take or leave the offer (hence the name of the game).

One might expect that the responder would accept any offer, no matter how small; after all, even a tiny portion of the good is better than nothing. And in fact that's what chimps do. But humans don't. Human responders have been repeatedly shown to reject any offer smaller than 20 percent — even though it's to their disadvantage to do so. The refusal is presumably intended to punish the proposer for his greed.

In this way chimpanzees turn out to be more rational economic agents than humans, who will walk away from an offer they deem unfair. And yet, *The Economist* points out, "a number of researchers in the field of human evolution think that a sense of fairness — and a willingness to punish the unfair even at some cost to oneself — is humanity's 'killer app.' It is what allows large social groups to form." Chimps are willing to punish actual thieves, but not perpetrators of unfairness. It seems that "the more sophisticated idea of fair shares, which underpins collaborative behaviour, appeared in the hominid line only after the ancestors of the two species split from one another."[5]

An impressive finding, but also a dismaying one. The moral order within is considerably less magisterial when viewed as a genetic glitch that happens to foster large-scale collective efforts. It's somewhat deflating to see our higher moral impulses as the operation of selfish genes rather than as the law of God imprinted on our hearts.

Of course, as the more exuberant defenders of scientistic humanism emphasize, we don't have to find these discoveries deflating. They are triumphs of the human mind; they mean that we understand the world (at least the visible world) in new and astonishing ways. And in fact we would probably be far more inclined to exult in our advances if they did not point to a grim conclusion: that the universe is blind and mechanical, we are infinitely small and alone in it, and our existence has no meaning.

Most theologians balk and wince when confronted with this possibility. Bonhoeffer does not. He is not afraid to ask the final, most dreadful question: "Even though there has been surrender on all secular problems, there still remain the so-called 'ultimate questions' — death, guilt, to which only 'God' can give an answer, and because of which we need God and the church and the pastor. So we live, in some degree, on these ultimate questions of humanity. But what if one day they no longer exist as such, if they too can be answered 'without God'?" Bonhoeffer showed no more courage, I believe, in resisting the Third Reich (for which he had been imprisoned) than he did in facing this issue.

Of course, it's one thing to pose such questions and quite another thing to answer them, and this Bonhoeffer fails to do. The letter trails off into theological niceties, which were no doubt interesting to his correspondent but seem irrelevant to the subject he has just raised. Another letter, written a month later, takes up the theme again:

> We cannot be honest unless we recognize that we have to live in the world *etsi deus non daretur* [even if God were not given to us]. And this is just what we do recognize — before God! ... The God who lets us live in the world without the working hypothesis of God is the God before whom we stand continually. Before God and with God we live without God. God lets

himself be pushed out of the world on to the cross. He is weak and powerless in the world, and that is precisely the way, the only way, in which he is with us and helps us.[6]

This passage combines two of the most distinctive aspects of Christianity through the centuries. On the one hand, for all its sins and enormities, Christianity has on countless occasions shown a relentless moral courage in embracing the suffering of the world: in feeding the poor, caring for the sick, and, like Bonhoeffer himself, opposing injustice. In this way, as Bonhoeffer might say, Christianity "is with us and helps us."

Alongside this formidable moral courage, on the other hand, we find a tremendous intellectual timidity and recalcitrance. It is simply unconvincing to say, "The God who lets us live in the world without the working hypothesis of God is the God before whom we stand continually." What does this mean? That we are supposed to believe in God because, in some mysterious and paradoxical way, we do not believe in him? This is a common tactic in Christianity, which has often taken refuge in paradox when it has found itself trapped in logical impossibilities. The most famous example is a remark by the church father Tertullian about the crucifixion of the Son of God: "Prorsus credibile est, quia ineptum est": "It is by all means to be believed because it is absurd."[7] For many centuries this approach worked — largely thanks to the emotional appeal (and political might) of Christianity rather than because of its innate plausibility — but as an answer to today's questions, it is not very helpful. Bonhoeffer, facing the Nazi hangmen, may have found solace in reflecting that God is asking us to live in a world in which we cannot believe in God. This is an impressive feat, but it does not necessarily enable us to take the same comfort.

Someone might object that this attitude is too rationalistic, that it doesn't do adequate justice to the mystery of the universe. Certainly there *are* genuine mysteries and paradoxes, and ignoring or denying them in some rationalistic fashion is mistaken. But this does not mean that one can evade every dilemma simply by calling it a paradox. Even Zen monks don't attempt to apply their koans outside the monastery.

Christianity consequently has made a habit of evading its own contradictions. Ironically, its great enemy, scientism, has done the same thing. Scientism, as I am using the term, is not science as such — which is a methodology rather than an ideology — but rather a pseudoreligion that has set up science as its god. Like conventional Christianity, scientism has its own baggage to hide and its own screen behind which it tries to stash this baggage. In the case of scientism, the baggage has to do with purpose, intent, and design in the universe. The screen it uses is blind chance and randomness.

Let's look at one of the more recent statements of this perspective, by the philosopher Daniel Dennett. Summarizing his refutation of the argument from design — the idea, first formulated by William Paley in his 1802 book *Natural Theology*, that the universe is so complex and intricate that it must have had a supremely intelligent designer — Dennett contends:

> When we looked through Darwin's eyes at the actual processes of design of which we and all the wonder of nature are the products to date, we found that Paley was right to see these effects as the result of a lot of design work, but we found a non-miraculous account of it: a massively parallel, and prodigiously wasteful, process of mindless, algorithmic design-trying, in which, however, the minimal increments of design have been thriftily husbanded, copied, and re-used over billions of years. . . .
>
> What is left behind is what the process, shuffling through eternity, mindlessly finds (when it finds anything): a timeless

Platonic possibility of order. That is, indeed, a thing of beauty, as mathematicians are forever exclaiming, *but it is not itself something intelligent but, wonder of wonders, something intelligible.*[8]

This is a fascinating passage. To say that the universe is not intelligent but intelligible has a certain rhetorical charm but glosses over one rather crucial question: where did the intelligence come from that is able to perceive the universe at all? If it developed out of mindless matter (as materialists argue), we are not told why or how. This was the conundrum I encountered while studying philosophy of mind at Oxford. Things have not changed much in the past thirty years. Even cognitive scientists still confess themselves to be at a loss about this question. In an October 2007 issue of *Scientific American*, neuroscientists Christof Koch and Susan Greenfield write, "Neuroscientists do not yet understand enough about the brain's inner workings to spell out exactly how consciousness *arises* from the chemical and electrical activity of neurons."[9]

What consciousness might be is one of the chief themes of this book, and I treat it in some detail. For now let's turn back to the first paragraph of Dennett's quotation, in which he says both that the process of evolution is *mindless* and that it involves *design*.

Let's grant Dennett's basic point: the old argument from design, the concept of a clockmaker God who fashioned the universe, is obsolete and unconvincing. This leaves us with an extremely strange dilemma: the concept of a design without a designer, or, if you prefer, an intent without anyone to intend it. And it is true that the idea of design hangs around scientism like a stray mongrel. Here is another passage from Dennett, in which he explains why we find sugar sweet: "Our sweet tooth is not just an accident or a pointless bug in an otherwise excellent system: it was *designed* to do the work it does, and if we underestimate its resourcefulness, its resistance to perturbation and suppression, our efforts to cope with it are apt to be counterproductive."[10]

Materialist philosophers insist that, when they mention design, it's simply a manner of speaking — a metaphor and nothing else. Another evangelist of scientism, Richard Dawkins, takes this tack in his 1976 book *The Selfish Gene*:

> We must not think of genes as conscious, purposeful agents. Blind natural selection, however, makes them behave rather as if they were purposeful, and it has been convenient, as a shorthand, to refer to genes in the language of purpose. For example, when we say "genes are trying to increase their numbers in future gene pools," what we really mean is "those genes which behave in such a way as to increase their numbers in future gene pools tend to be the genes whose effects we see in the world." ... The idea of purpose is only a metaphor, but we have already seen what a fruitful metaphor it is in the case of genes. We have even used words like "selfish" and "ruthless" of genes, knowing full well that it is only a figure of speech.[11]

Of course it's legitimate to use figures of speech, and they are bound to resemble what they model only to an imperfect degree. But what kind of theory is it that constantly uses certain metaphors as integral parts of its explanation while at the same time denying those same metaphors? Even to speak of "behav[ing] in such a way as to increase their numbers" implies some purpose and intent, in the behavior if nothing else. In most of his book, Dawkins goes much further. The British philosopher Mary Midgley chides him for his "habitual rhetoric in elevating the gene from its real position as a humble bit of goo within cells to a malign and powerful agent."[12]

Even if we can and must remove the clockmaker God from our explanations of the universe, it is not so easy to take away intelligence or design. The apostles of scientism insist over and over again that the forces of nature — natural selection, genes, "algo-rithmic design-trying," and so on — are mindless, but they can't even speak coherently about these things without using the con-cept of mind in some form.

It's said that, to a man who has only a hammer, everything looks like a nail. By the same token, to a philosopher armed only with Occam's razor, every proposition looks like something to cut. Standard evolutionary theory wants to trim away the supposedly unnecessary hypothesis of intelligence in the origin of species, but it is then left holding only, in Dennett's words, "a massively par-allel, and prodigiously wasteful, process of mindless, algorithmic design-trying" to explain everything. This move may not be as simple and elegant as it might first appear. After all, cases com-monly cited as proofs of the evolution of species by natural selec-tion often don't involve the development of new species at all. Consider the celebrated case of the peppered moth in the industrial Midlands of nineteenth-century England. Before the Industrial Revolution, these moths were light gray with dark gray speckles, a color that served as camouflage when the moths rested on the bark of trees. After industrial pollution turned many of these trunks black, the peppered moth adapted by changing color: most of the moths were now dark gray with light gray speckles. No less an authority than the BBC website hands down the word from Cambridge professor Mike Majerus: "The rise and fall of the pep-pered moth . . . provides the proof of evolution."[13] Does it? It *does* prove adaptation by natural selection, but it doesn't prove that such adaptation produces new species; after all, both light- and dark-gray moths remain part of the same species, *Biston betularia*.[14] So much for the elegance and economy of evolutionary theory. As Mary Midgley writes, "False economy is very common among people who rely too readily on it. As we are seeing, extravagance is not eliminated merely by becoming anti-religious, and thoughts which are designed to be sternly reductive often compensate by strange, illicit expansions elsewhere. In fact when we encounter a specially harsh reduction, officially launched in the name of parsimony, our first question should be: 'and what are these savings being used to pay for?' "[15]

Here, then, is the strange impasse we face at the beginning of the twenty-first century — theologians who cannot quite believe in God, and militant materialists who cannot quite do without intelligence, design, or purpose. There have been many attempts at finding a middle ground. One of the best known of these can be found in the work of John Shelby Spong, a retired Episcopal bishop who has published several books calling on Christianity to update its shopworn worldview. Indeed Spong equates his own program with Bonhoeffer's "religionless Christianity."[16] In his book *A New Christianity for a New World*, Spong writes:

> Could we not begin to envision a transcendence that enters our life but also calls us beyond the limits of our humanity, not toward an external being but toward the Ground of All Being including our own, a transcendence that calls to a new humanity? Is there not a new maturity that can be claimed by human life when we cease the search for a supernatural being who will parent us, take care of us, watch over and protect us? Is there not a new human dignity that can be found in the rejection of those groveling patterns of our past through which we attempted to please the theistic deity in the early years of evolutionary history? In place of that groveling, are we not now able to open ourselves in new ways to discover the Ground of Being that is met and known in the self that is emerging as expanded consciousness?[17]

Finally, it would appear, someone is striking a balance between reactionary atheism and naive theism. To speak of a Ground of

All Being instead of a petulant personal deity would seem to be not only more rational but more profoundly experiential than the stale Christianity of sermons and liturgies. Such classics as William James's *Varieties of Religious Experience*, Evelyn Underhill's *Mysticism*, and Aldous Huxley's *Perennial Philosophy* offer many testimonies to the profound truth of this Ground as witnessed and felt by the great mystics of all ages.

Nor are these experiences confined to believers. The British philosopher A. J. Ayer, the doyen of logical positivism, was such a relentless atheist that the novelist W. Somerset Maugham in his last days summoned Ayer to reassure him that there was no life after death. In a London hospital in 1988, Ayer's heart stopped for four minutes. In that time, he later wrote, he saw a red light and became "aware that this light was responsible for the government of the universe." The experience did not change his atheism, but "slightly weakened my conviction that my genuine death — which is due fairly soon — will be the end of me, though I continue to hope it will be." Ayer did in fact die a year later.[18]

Even if we attempt to view God impersonally — as the Ground of All Being or the light that governs the universe — the matter is not quite so simple. The human race does more things before its gods than merely grovel. For those who believe in him, God is an ever-present support, a shelter in times of trouble, an eternal rock in which we can hide ourselves — the hymnbooks and psalters offer us countless images. Curiously, the human race needs God in this sense more than it ever has. In the old cosmologies, the cosmos was small and man loomed large in it; today we can no longer take pride in our own centrality. Feeling more alone and helpless in the universe, we are consequently more in need of a loving entity who will watch over us. An impersonal Ground of All Being will not give us this comfort.

A still more perplexing problem with a religion centered on a Ground of All Being is that it does not answer scientistic objections any better than does the notion of a personal God. After all, if we can explain the workings of the universe without a divine craftsman, we can do so equally well without a Ground of All Being. There is no place for either one in the allegedly flawless causal chain of the universe. Although the experience of this Ground by mystics, visionaries, and even atheists constitutes strong evidence for its existence, this evidence is necessarily "anecdotal," and science has complacently ignored it — or has attempted to explain it away reductionistically as merely a change in brain states.

Here lies the postmodern discomfort. At the dawn of the third millennium, religion, science, philosophy, and mysticism remain a hopelessly jumbled patchwork that no one can fit together. The solution has been attempted so often, with such inadequate results, that it seems presumptuous to try again. And yet I think an answer is possible. Like most good solutions to apparently complex quandaries, it is both self-consistent and comparatively simple. It does not do violence to the findings of science, and I believe that, if it is taken up to a certain point, even the more strident materialists may find it acceptable. Taken beyond this point, it offers a way of approaching a great deal of experience that science does not want to bother with.

If this solution had, like Athena, sprung solely out of my own head, one might have reason to be suspicious of it. But I believe it is implicit — and sometimes explicit — in the mystical and esoteric traditions of the world (which are remarkably similar for being so far-flung). What I propose is not so much a radical new theory as a fresh perspective based on some extremely ancient traditions. I have proposed aspects of this view in my previous books, but it is necessary to flesh it out further in order to apply it more broadly.

The central concept in any portrait of an intelligible universe is *consciousness*. And yet consciousness is not easy to define. As we've already seen, it's an entity elusive even to neurologists, who have been poking and prodding the brain for decades. Philosophers do no better: you can read any number of books purportedly explaining consciousness and come away scarcely any better informed. Practically all the current discussion of the topic amounts to a sort of evasion, saying that the brain *affects* consciousness — a fact that was discussed as far back as 400 BC, in *On the Sacred Disease*, the Hippocratic treatise on epilepsy.[19] But how the brain *produces* consciousness — what philosophers call the "mind-brain problem" or the "mind-body problem" — remains as opaque as ever. The philosopher Colin McGinn has even argued that the problem of consciousness is fundamentally insoluble, leading some of his critics to deride him for his "mysterianism."[20] And I'm speaking here purely in terms of human consciousness; how this might relate to nonhuman consciousness, divine or otherwise, is even more puzzling.

Let me begin, then, by proposing an extremely simple but extremely fertile definition: consciousness is that which relates self and other. In terms of human cognition, this seems obvious. The sense of a self, an *I* present *here* versus an *other* present *there*, is central to the concept of consciousness. Knowing that I am present in my study, sitting at a desk in front of a computer, is essential to my being conscious here and now. If I were utterly oblivious to these things, I could not be said to be conscious at all, as, for example, during a state of dreamless sleep.

As soon as we've said this much, however, we realize that consciousness admits any number of degrees and gradations. While dreaming, you are not aware of the physical world, but some awareness still remains: there is the self that is a character in the dream, set off against other characters and settings and objects that also appear. This is not waking consciousness, but still it is consciousness of a kind. If we go further into dreamless sleep, there is apparently no consciousness of any kind — and yet below the surface the distinction of self and other does remain. After all, one of the most universally prescribed remedies for illness is sleep. Sleep, even and perhaps especially in its dreamless form, helps the "self" of the body fight off the "other" of the pathogens.

We can go further. Anyone with even the slightest experience of animals knows that they too are capable of relating self and other. Dogs and cats can't reason except in the most rudimentary sense, and yet they have emotional lives that are enough like our own to be more or less understandable. Can we, then, say they are conscious, not as we are, but conscious nonetheless? Or should we say, with Descartes, that they are mere automatons? Not many thinkers have wanted to agree with the great philosopher on this point. What about more primitive creatures, going down as far as plants and even protozoans? We may be fairly sure that they don't engage in Cartesian introspections, but their fierce attachment to life, to perpetuating their own existence, indicates that they too have some sense of themselves over and against an external world. As we have already learned from Richard Dawkins, one could make the same argument about the naked genes themselves.

Like so many of the discoveries of the past few centuries, these insights seem to erode the human sense of uniqueness and privilege in being the sole possessor of the magnificent gift called consciousness, but there are some consolations. The problem of human consciousness becomes less confounding if we see it not as something sprung mysteriously out of nowhere but rather as a stage on a continuum. Moreover, if it is taken to heart, this outlook may even help mitigate the feeling of isolation and separation that is the unhappy side effect of our arrogant sense of uniqueness.

Where, then, do we draw the line? At inanimate things? That apparently inanimate objects contain a rudimentary form of consciousness has long been known to the philosophy of India. The British scholar Sir John Woodroffe explains its views:

> The manifestation of consciousness is more or less limited as ascent is made from the mineral to man. In the mineral world Cit [consciousness] manifests as the lowest form of sentiency evidenced by reflex response to stimuli, and that physical consciousness which is called in the West atomic memory. The sentiency of plants is more developed, though it is . . . a dormant consciousness. This is further manifested in those micro-organisms which are intermediate stages between the vegetable and animal worlds, and have a psychic life of their own. In the animal world consciousness becomes more centralized and complex, reaching its fullest development in man, who possesses all the psychic functions such as cognition, perception, feeling and will. Behind all these particular changing forms of sentiency or consciousness is the one formless, changeless Cit as it is in itself.[21]

This ostensibly Eastern idea appears in the West as well, sometimes in unexpected places. Here is an excerpt from an 1890 interview with Thomas Edison by George Parsons Lathrop:

> "I do not believe," [Edison] said, "that matter is inert, acted upon by an outside force. To me it seems that every atom is possessed by a certain amount of primitive intelligence. Look at the thousands of ways in which atoms of hydrogen combine with those of other elements, forming the most diverse substances. Do you mean to say that they do this without intelligence? . . . Gathered together in certain forms, the atoms constitute animals of the lower orders. Finally they combine in man, who represents the total intelligence of all the atoms."

"But where does this intelligence come from originally?" I asked.

"From some power greater than ourselves."[22]

Restating the point, we could say that a hydrogen atom "knows" how to recognize an oxygen atom and, under certain circumstances, how to combine with it to form water. It can, in a manner of speaking, perceive something outside of it and relate to it; it is, in a rudimentary sense, conscious. If an atom could not take a stance in the physical world and draw some kind of line between itself and what is not itself, it could not exist. Perhaps this is the secret of those tenuous submolecular particles about which today's physics speculates so imaginatively. They seem to flash in and out of existence, or, in certain instances, not to exist at all unless they are observed. It is as if their sense of themselves is so frail and ambiguous that it takes an external perceiver to bring them into being, much as the eighteenth-century Anglo-Irish bishop and philosopher George Berkeley claimed that the universe would vanish if God were not there to perceive it.

I must digress here to say one thing. Many current thinkers who have grappled with the subject of consciousness have invoked the findings of twentieth-century physics as some kind of proof of their ideas. I don't intend to do this myself; I'm not trying to make grandiose claims about "quantum consciousness" or anything of that sort. Several years ago, interviewing Larry Dossey, MD, author of *Healing Words* and *Space, Time, and Medicine*, I asked him about the relation of consciousness to quantum physics. He replied:

> My verdict is out. I often refer to quantum theories, not because they're going to give us an explanation for what happens at the human level, but simply because they provide a kind of permission to think about nonlocality in the first place. . . .

It could be that something here might explain how distant effects of consciousness work; we just don't know. But I object to people talking about quantum psychology, quantum prayer, quantum spirituality. We're dragooned with the quantum metaphor. And most people do not use it as a metaphor but think it's much more than that. I personally don't believe it is. It may turn out that way, but we're a long way from that now.[23]

Similarly, the parapsychologist Lawrence LeShan writes:

We can decide that, since the science of quantum mechanics is so full of mysterious concepts, the "explanation" of psi [psychic phenomena] must lie there. Thus there is really no problem; everything about psi has already been explained by quantum science, or will be very soon. Forty years ago, I was one of the people who started the idea that psi could be explained in terms of quantum mechanics or relativity theory. I now believe that we were wrong, and I regret my part in it. Dignity, love, loyalty, awe, and psi must be dealt with on their own terms in a science built on these observables, not one built on the observables of subatomic particles.[24]

Dossey's and LeShan's points are important and often overlooked. The human mind forges many chains for its own enslavement. These include metaphors that have overstepped their proper bounds. Scientific discoveries as "proofs" of spiritual truths seem to be among the most common form of this abuse at present. To say what I am saying here, on the other hand, does not rely on the truths of a particular scientific worldview — Newtonian, Einsteinian, or any other. After all, to speak of an object of any kind is to delineate it from the background of the rest of the world, to set it off as *itself* and not something other. And if things are to exist objectively and not merely as subjective impressions in one's head, they must stake out their own place in relation to the universe.

That is, they must take a stance as *self* as opposed to the *other* that constitutes the rest of reality. So they are endowed with consciousness, however unlike our own it may be.

If we grant all this, we are left asking precisely what the relation is between self and other, between consciousness and experience, between "I" and the world. This is the most subtle and profound question that we can pose, because to go beyond this point renders us unable to say anything at all. To explore this issue, we might best start off not with science or philosophy but with myth. And one of the most powerful myths to address this relationship between consciousness and experience is the strange and haunting tale, well-known in India, obscure in the West, of the game of dice that the god Shiva plays with his consort, Parvati.

CHAPTER TWO

THE GAME OF CONSCIOUSNESS

One day the embraces of the Hindu god Shiva and his consort, Parvati, who have spent eternity rapt in lovemaking, are interrupted by a sinister yogi named Narada. Narada says he can show them something that is even more delightful than love. It is a game of dice — an ancestor of today's Parcheesi.

Intrigued by his offer, the divine couple begin to play. Each of them cheats as much as possible, but no matter how long they play, the outcome is always the same: <u>Shiva loses and Parvati wins.</u> Shiva may have the advantage for a round or two, but he can never win a game.

At one point Shiva is ahead; he has won a couple of Parvati's jewels, enraging her. Noticing that the angrier she grows, the more beautiful she becomes, he coaxes her into continuing. Parvati agrees to play if Shiva will wager his chief attributes: his trident, the crescent moon, and a pair of earrings.

Of course Shiva plays and loses. But he refuses to accept this fact; after all, he is Shiva, the lord of the universe. "No living being can overcome me," he tells her. She replies, "No living being can overcome you, it's true — except me." In spite, she leaves him. She takes not only the trident and the moon and the earrings but a pair of snakes and even his last item of clothing, his loincloth.

Shiva is not troubled by this outcome. He withdraws to the wilderness and leads the life of an ascetic, free from the preoccupations of the world, meditating in solitary peace. Parvati, on the other hand, feels lonely and frustrated without him. Intent on winning him back, she takes the form of a lovely tribeswoman (an untouchable in the Hindu caste system) with red lips, a graceful neck, and magnificent full breasts. She is so beautiful that even the bees in the forest are overcome with love.

Shiva, roused from his meditation by the noise of the bees, sees Parvati in the guise of the tribeswoman and is overcome with desire for her. Coquettishly she says, "I am looking for a husband who is omniscient, who is free and fulfills all needs, who is free of mutations and is the lord of the worlds."

Shiva says, "I am that one."

Parvati replies, "You shouldn't talk to me that way. I happen to know that you have a wife who won your devotion by many austerities, and you left her in a flash. Besides, you are an ascetic, living free from duality."

"Even so, I want you."

Parvati says that he must ask permission of her father, Himalaya, the lord of the mountain chain. Shiva approaches him, but Himalaya says, "This is not right. You should not be asking me. You are the one who gives everything in all the worlds."

At this point Narada reappears and tells Shiva, "Listen. Infatuation with women always leads to mockery."

"You're right," Shiva replies. "I have been a fool." And Shiva withdraws to a remote part of the universe where even yogis cannot go.

At this point Narada convinces Parvati and Himalaya to implore Shiva to return, and they do so by praising him lavishly. Mollified, Shiva comes back, and he and Parvati resume their reign in unity.[1]

Contrary to Einstein, this myth seems to be saying that God not only plays dice with the universe but constantly loses. Why should Shiva, the lord of the universe, be lured into indulging in a form of strip Parcheesi? How can he lose? Who is his consort? Why does she win?

By now it's common knowledge that myth contains meaning that is hard if not impossible to convey in ordinary discursive language. There are no doubt different levels of meaning, each with its own import. I will try to tease out the most significant aspects of this story.

Shiva represents consciousness — what I have been calling variously *purusha*, "I," or "I am" — that is, consciousness in a sense much more universal than mere human awareness. Parvati represents *prakriti*, the *contents* of consciousness: experience in all its forms, internal and external, what esoteric Christianity calls the "world." At the beginning of the myth they are locked in union. There is no distinction between consciousness and its contents. Therefore there is no world. The Hindus call this state *pralaya*, the state of primordial sleep that prevailed before the universe bestirred itself to manifest. The Hindu scripture known as the Rig Veda describes it:

> Then [before the beginning]
> there was neither death nor no-death,
> no sign of night or day.

> The One breathed, breathless,
> through its own impulsion,
> and there was no Other of any kind.[2]

Note that it's precisely the absence of the "Other" that characterizes this primal repose. The dice game, introduced by Narada, the personification of discord, symbolizes the beginning of manifestation. No manifestation can exist without a distinction between self and other. But as I suggested in the previous chapter, this distinction is not the bailiwick only of conscious subjects, such as we imagine ourselves to be. It is the property of everything, because, as I indicated, even an atom or electron must have some sense of itself simply to cohere at all. It must perceive an other in order to distinguish itself from that other and so maintain a stable existence.

As weirdly mystical as this idea may sound, it is occasionally echoed even by the philosophers who are most seminal to the contemporary scientific worldview. One example comes from *An Essay Concerning Human Understanding* by John Locke, one of the grandfathers of the philosophy of "nothing but." Although Locke made this statement almost as an aside, it would help inspire the whole trend of philosophical materialism in the coming centuries:

> We have the *Ideas* of Matter and *Thinking*, but possibly shall never be able to know, whether any mere material Being thinks, or no; it being impossible for us, by the contemplation of our own *Ideas*, without revelation, to discover, whether Omnipotency has not given to some Systems of Matter fitly disposed, a power to perceive and think, or else joined and fixed to Matter so disposed, a thinking immaterial Substance: It being, in respect of our Notions, not much more remote from our Comprehension to conceive, that GOD can, if he pleases, superadd to Matter a Faculty of Thinking, than that he should superadd to it another Substance with a faculty of Thinking. . . . For I see

no contradiction in it, that the first eternal thinking Being should, if he pleased, give to certain Systems of created sense-less matter, put together as he thinks fit, some degrees of sense, perception, and thought.[3]

Locke himself, later in the same book, argues against the idea that matter can be conscious.[4] Nonetheless, it was his suggestion that matter could possess "some degrees of sense, perception, and thought" that would eventually lead to the attempt to equate the mind with the functioning of the brain or to characterize the mind as a mere epiphenomenon, a side effect, of brain activity.

The materialists can't have it both ways. They cannot argue *both* that consciousness is implicit in matter *and* that matter is mindless. To do this, they would have to show how consciousness arises out of unconscious matter, and this is exactly what none of them have done. As one psychologist remarked, brain activity resembles the mind about as much as a telephone number resembles its subscriber.

The fundamental dynamic of reality, then, is that of Shiva and Parvati: consciousness, or self, in all its forms, and experience, or the *other*, in all its forms. After all, if consciousness consists of the ability to relate self and other, this polarity is and must be primary. If there is no self and other, there is no universe.*

In the previous chapter I pointed out that some philosophers, notably Colin McGinn, have said that the problem of consciousness is fundamentally insoluble. McGinn is certainly right to the extent that it has not been solved by Western philosophy, whose

---

* This comment may arouse some doubt in Buddhists, one of whose primary doctrines is *anatta*, or "no-self." I discuss this point further in chapter 6, but for now let me say that this "self-other" distinction is fundamental to the universe, even if, from a Buddhist point of view, both this type of consciousness and this universe are delusory.

explanations have come to resemble a windup toy that continues to march even though it's run up against a wall. But if we see con-sciousness as the capacity to relate self and other, the difficulty begins to diminish. Consciousness is now revealed as being present anywhere and everywhere in the universe; our own consciousness is simply one particular, and not necessarily privileged, form of it. It is true that we can't say much more about consciousness than that it consists of this relation of self to other, but then we can't say *anything* about entities that have no sense of this relation — that is, which have no boundaries by which to define themselves at all.

These observations lead to another: Nothing in manifest exis-tence is *absolutely* a self or an other. They are merely matters of perspective. A hydrogen atom has some consciousness, demon-strated by its ability to recognize an atom of oxygen and interact with it under certain circumstances to form water and other com-pounds. From its point of view, it is a self and the oxygen atom is the other. To the oxygen atom, exactly the opposite is the case: the hydrogen atom is the other, just as I am other to you and you are other to me. This fact indicates that the relation between self and other, between "I" and the world outside, is a constant, dynamic interplay for all entities at all scales and levels of complexity. A metaphor for this is the game known as Othello, or Reversal, which employs disks that are black on one side and white on the other. Each player takes turns setting them down on a grid, and the player who has more disks of his own color on the board at the end of the game wins. If, say, you are the black player and you manage to cap a line of white disks with your own black disks at both ends, the whole line of white disks flip over to black. In the course of the game, whole lines of disks flip from white to black and back again. This process hints at the ever-shifting reversal of self and other that prevails in the universe at all levels.

But to return to the dice game of the myth, where does it fit in? And why does Shiva always lose?

Shiva represents what one of the Upanishads calls the "seer of seeing."[5] Seeing in all its forms — that is, consciousness — imparts existence to the world. <u>Nothing exists unless it *is seen*.</u> Paradoxically, this includes Shiva's own attributes. They do not, strictly speaking, belong to consciousness, which in its pure form has no attributes; it simply sees. (This may help explain why philosophers are frustrated in their attempts to define it.) Any qualities that we can ascribe to consciousness are immediately *seen*; they are part of the world; and the world is Parvati. And so Parvati always wins. Her victory strips Shiva down to his pure, naked essence, which is seeing alone. For all the possible throws of the dice — that is, for all the possible directions manifestation can take — Shiva will always lose.

Nevertheless, Shiva takes his defeat with aplomb and simply retreats to the forest. <u>That is to say, consciousness can detach itself from its experience; it can free itself from its own contents. This detachment is the goal of many forms of meditation. It suggests why Shiva is characterized as an ascetic.</u>

Consider your own experience now. Most likely you are not aware of yourself, except as part of a vague background. But if you bring your attention to yourself, you can feel yourself as an "I" having experiences. Many of these are sensory: this room, this chair, this book. You can go still deeper. You can be aware of your thoughts and feelings as they pass over the screen of your awareness (which is generally easier to do if you close your eyes). <u>If you can be aware of even these most private and intimate thoughts as somehow "other," then where is the "I"? Who or what is it? It has no attributes as such, no qualities; it simply sees.</u> Hence the Hindu sage Sri Ramana Maharshi said that the question <u>"Who am I?,"</u> taken back far enough, will lead to enlightenment.

Enlightenment as customarily conceived is a somewhat shadowy concept. About all one can say of it is that it is a higher state of consciousness than we're accustomed to or for that matter usually believe possible. In light of the ideas I've sketched out, however, we might be able to say a bit more. The consciousness that causes the world to arise is common to all things, human and nonhuman, animate and inanimate; there is nothing that does not possess it to some degree. But we almost never experience it in this universal way. On the contrary, it is always *me*, *my* consciousness, fenced in with rigid lines to insulate it from all others. It is precisely this rigid distinction, which is to a great extent artificial and delusory, that constitutes the sleep of man. In the words of Sri Ramana Maharshi: *"Only one Consciousness, equally distributed everywhere. You through delusion give It unequal distribution. No distribution, no everywhere."*[6] Or, as the Greek sage Heraclitus says, "Consciousness is common to all, but most people live as if they had their own private minds."[7]

Enlightenment, it would seem, lies precisely in the recognition of this truth, not through the mediation of concepts but directly and intuitively. It may and often does come in an instant. Such insight may be dazzling for the one who experiences it, but it may also not be. For many people, I suspect, it comes "as a thief in the night," and they cast it aside in the belief that enlightenment means that the heavens open and one sees ladders full of angels going up and down, or that one becomes instantly omniscient.

In any event, this experience of insight — whether we call it enlightenment, illumination, gnosis, or something else — marks a fundamental shift in an individual's orientation. Afterward she is not necessarily immune to the vicissitudes of life: joys and sorrows and aches and pains come as they always have. But in a subtle way they have lost their hold on her. They are no longer absolutes, to be taken at face value. She is aware of a dimension of mind in herself that is above the passing thrills and irritations of existence. This is supernally real and can never be taken away, and so is to be valued above all things. "The kingdom of heaven is like unto treasure hid in a field: the which when a man hath found, he hideth, and for joy thereof goeth and selleth all that he hath, and buyeth that field" (Matthew 13:44).[8]

From a certain point of view, the spiritual path can be divided into two parts. In the first part, the individual senses that what we customarily take to be reality is no such thing, that there is something much more to be found. He looks and looks for it; he reads, studies, meditates, goes to hear the lectures of wise and holy people, and undergoes many exercises and disciplines and austerities. Then, in an instant, bidden or unbidden, the realization comes, whether through the whack of a Zen master's stick or in a flash of insight that occurs during a humdrum chore. After this, nothing can be the same again. Even the spiritual path is no longer the same. The individual is not omniscient or omnipotent, but he now knows something real and true. Study and practice also become reoriented. They now are aimed not at producing this realization but at stabilizing it and integrating it into all levels of his life and mind.

Such a person even finds that his attitude toward spiritual literature undergoes a distinctive change. He begins to discern — among the innumerable books and ideas available in the marketplace — those that come from genuine knowing and those that do not. The difference is subtle but remarkably sharp. He may even pick up a book, glance through it, and find himself saying about the author, "Ah! He *almost* knows!" Preoccupation with doctrinal orthodoxies, the truth of "my" religion over all others, and an arrogant contempt for other points of view almost always indicate that the writer does *not* know.

What then of Parvati? She is the world, the sum total of all experience. I use the word *experience* because it seems to be the most all-encompassing of the terms available. Your experience, your world, includes not only your thoughts and emotions and sensations but your memories, dreams, and imaginations. Present-day knowledge has a refined set of criteria for determining which things are defined as "real" and which are not (I spell these out later), but all of your experience is real *as experience*. If you are delirious with fever and start to hallucinate, the delusory images you see have no objective existence, but even so you are still experiencing something.

I might have picked a term other than *experience*, one that might be more evocative of previous philosophical outlooks. Had I chosen *representation*, for example, what I am saying would immediately reveal its affinities with the thought of Arthur Schopenhauer. (The equivalent term in Schopenhauer's German is *Vorstellung*.) Schopenhauer writes:

> That the *objective existence* of things is conditioned by a representer of them, and that consequently the objective world exists only *as representation*, is no hypothesis, still less a peremptory pronouncement, or even a paradox put forward for the sake of debate and argument. On the contrary, it is the surest and simplest truth, and a knowledge of it is rendered more difficult only by the fact that it is indeed too simple, and that not everyone has sufficient power of reflection to go back to the first elements of his consciousness of things.[9]

Schopenhauer, of all the great Western philosophers, was the only one who revealed any deep or genuine understanding of the philosophy of India. And yet in our civilization, his philosophy and others like it, which are broadly grouped under the rubric of "idealism," have always occupied a minority position. Why?

Sometimes these theories run aground on the problem of solipsism. They may appear to reduce the entire universe to *my* private experience — a counterintuitive conclusion. After all, I seem to be moving around among other beings very much like me, who have or say they are having experiences very much like mine; why should I assume that I alone am a conscious subject?

The idea that I am the only being having conscious experience is so utterly untenable that practically no one has seriously tried to maintain it. Curiously, however, it's an assumption we automatically make about a significant part of our experience: the dream world. In our dreams we encounter a reality that is in many ways similar to waking life: there are objects, places, even people. But we automatically assume we are the only genuine conscious subjects in this world. Some years ago I had a lucid dream in which I was sitting on a seashore. Next to me was an eighteen-year-old boy. I became aware I was dreaming, and when I shared this insight with my companion, he said indignantly, "You mean you think I'm a *dream character*?" He was insulted.

The interplay of dreaming and waking life is so mysterious and evanescent that, if we reflect on it, we may end up repeating the commonplace sentiment that "life is a dream." Or, like certain Hindus, we might decide that the only reason we think waking life is real, while dreams are not, is that we spend more of our time in the former. Some Tibetan Buddhists practice a rigorous yoga that is intended to maintain an unbroken line of consciousness from the waking to the dream state, so as to reveal the essentially empty nature of all phenomena. Even if we don't go this far, if we have done a certain amount of introspection we might reach a conclusion echoed in esoteric teaching: at times in our dreams we stray beyond the boundaries of our private imaginings and enter a world that, although it is not real in the customary sense, has a certain subtle substantiality and operates according to laws that are in many respects like those of waking life.

In any event, Schopenhauer's position presents other problems as well: for example, if all the universe is representation, what was there before there was anyone to perceive it? Much of this argument is based on an unconscious anthropomorphism — assuming that our consciousness is the only kind. or that consciousness deserves the name only to the degree that it resembles our own. Schopenhauer again:

> Animals existed before men, fishes before land animals, plants before fishes, and the inorganic before that which is organic; consequently the original mass had to go through a long series of changes before the first eye could be opened. And yet the existence of this whole world remains for ever dependent on that first eye that opened, were it even that of an insect. For such an eye necessarily brings about knowledge, for which and in which alone the whole world is, and without which it is not even conceivable. The world is entirely representation, and as such requires the knowing subject as the supporter of its existence.[10]

Schopenhauer is willing to push his definition of a "knowing subject" at least to the extent of including insects. Nonetheless, it sounds as if the world did not exist before there was someone to perceive it, even if that someone had six legs. Yet as Schopenhauer knew, the world existed for immeasurable eons before the appearance of anything he would regard as a knowing subject. He tries to evade this difficulty by saying that representation belongs not to things as they are — what, following Kant, he calls the "thing in itself" — but only to things as they are perceived. Only will belongs to the thing in itself. And will has always existed: it is eternal, beyond time, space, and causality, like the Forms of Plato's philosophy (with which Schopenhauer explicitly equates his concept of will).[11] There was always will, but there was representation only after the emergence of a knowing subject.

This is a problematic view, not least because it implies that time, space, and causality (which are characteristics of representation rather than of will) did not exist before the appearance of a knowing subject. This is hard to credit. Even if we stretch Schopenhauer's concept of the knowing subject to include any form of life, life appeared on earth somewhat under 3.8 billion years ago, while the universe is currently believed to be around 13.7 billion years old.

The other major Western philosopher to hold that the world is entirely composed of experience was Bishop Berkeley. According to him, objects consist of nothing more than a congeries of impressions registered by a conscious mind. "A certain colour, taste, smell, figure and consistence having been observed to go together, are accounted one distinct thing, signified by the name apple," he writes. And nothing exists unless it is perceived: "Their [that is, objective things'] *esse* [being] is *percipi* [to be perceived], nor is it possible they should have any existence out of the minds or thinking things which perceive them."[12]

The obvious objection is this: Does a tree cease to exist when I turn away from it, only to reappear when I turn back? Clearly not. Berkeley replies, "When I deny sensible things an existence out of the mind, I do not mean my mind in particular, but all minds. Now, it is plain that they have an existence exterior to my mind; since I find them by experience to be independent of it. There is therefore some other Mind wherein they exist, during the intervals between the times of my perceiving them; as likewise they did before my birth, and would do after my supposed annihilation. . . . It necessarily follows there is an *omnipresent eternal Mind,* which knows and comprehends all things."[13] For Berkeley, who was an Anglican bishop, this omnipresent eternal Mind is God.

Berkeley's system no doubt reconciled faith and reason for his own thinking, but most philosophers since his time have not been so convinced. Berkeley's God looks very much like a deus ex machina: having decided that to be is to be perceived, Berkeley needs to come up with someone who is looking when no one else is. Like Schopenhauer's, this approach stumbles on its anthropomorphism: the consciousness that perceives has to be humanlike. Since the nonhuman and inanimate realms possess no consciousness of any sort, this supreme, transcendent intelligence has to be that of a personal God.

Both Schopenhauer's and Berkeley's views have much to recommend them. The world *is* the sum total of that which is experienced, but not just by human subjects or, for that matter, by living creatures. Consciousness, the capacity for recognition and response, is embedded in all things, and nothing could exist without it. As noted in the previous chapter, Edison says, "Look at the thousands of ways in which atoms of hydrogen combine with those of other elements, forming the most diverse substances. Do you mean to say that they do this without intelligence?" Intelligence, or, shall we say, consciousness, is embedded in all things, and nothing could exist without it. By taking this step, we need not stretch our imaginations to conceive of how a substantial world could exist before the arrival of a "knowing subject"; nor must we invoke the artificial notion of a transcendent deity who exists merely to keep an eye on things. Consciousness and experience, "I" and the world — or "heaven" and "earth," as they are sometimes called symbolically — are revealed as the fundamental axes of reality.

We then find ourselves asking what is real. The answers to this question over the centuries can be broadly divided into two types. One is the mystical view that only what is eternal and unchanging is real. Although this idea may look highly "Eastern" to us today, it

Intelligence as consciousness

actually has a long and distinguished ancestry in Western philosophy — for example, in Plato. He discusses it in a number of his works, but the best-known account appears in *The Republic*, where he contends that, in the world of sensory appearances, everything is relative. Something is beautiful in one context, ugly in another; an act that is moral in one set of circumstances is immoral in another, and so on. None of these things, then, can be counted as really having these characteristics; in a sense they both do and do not have them. As Plato's mouthpiece, Socrates, says, "It is impossible to form a stable conception of any of them as either being what it is, or not being what it is, or being both, or neither. . . . The welter of things which the masses conventionally regard as beautiful and so on mill around somewhere between unreality and perfect reality."[14]

There is a semantic difficulty here that is often overlooked. The word in Plato's Greek that is usually translated as "reality" is <u>ousía, literally, "being."</u> If we understand this point, Plato's reasoning becomes much clearer. How can you say something "is" when you find that, in respect to anything you can say about it, it both "is" and "is not"? How can you say something *is* green when it looks green in one light and yellow or gray in another?

Nonetheless, the English terms are *real* and *reality*, and their etymology suggests how we native speakers of English view the matter. These words derive from the Latin *res*, "thing." <u>In English, reality is inextricably bound up with thingness. W</u>e see as much in the term *real estate*. When you buy a house, you don't care that the materials composing it were not a house in the past and someday in the (let us hope remote) future will no longer be a house. Nor do you care that in a sense the house both is and is not white. What matters is that it is a house you can see and touch and live in now, and that the plumbing is in good shape.

Property matters aside, in the day-to-day world there are, I would suggest, five criteria that something has to satisfy in order for us to accept it as real:

1. It must be *perceptible to the senses in a stereoscopic way*. That is, it must resemble what it is to all the senses and from all angles. Once when I was young, I was in my room around twilight, when I glanced across the hall into my father's bedroom and saw what looked like a dead mouse in the middle of the floor. I was puzzled, because I knew we didn't have mice in the house. I looked at the object for some time, trying to figure out what it might be, but no matter how hard I tried, I could not see it as anything other than a mouse. Finally I got up to take a closer look at it. I found it was a crumpled-up piece of tissue paper that had missed the wastebasket. In this case, what had looked like a mouse proved, from a more comprehensive point of view, to be otherwise. Consequently it was not really a mouse.

2. The object must have a certain *stability*. It can't appear and vanish or change form in unpredictable ways.

3. It must be *publicly accessible*. Anyone who is present must be able to perceive it. Anyone here principally means a sane, rational, sober adult. The testimony of children, the insane, and people who are intoxicated is viewed with much more suspicion.

4. It must be observed *in waking life*. Objects in dreams may appear to have many of the characteristics I've described, but even so they are not accounted as real.

5. It must obey our *preconceptions* about what is and is not possible. If you say you saw something that is supposed not to exist, your testimony will be seriously doubted. You may even doubt your own senses, the power of whose evidence is often weaker than that of our preconceptions.

Anything that fits these criteria will generally be taken as real. If something fails to satisfy even some of these requirements, it will raise doubts. Take the typical sighting of a ghost. The apparition may not be entirely stable: it may appear and disappear suddenly. It may not seem substantial to all the senses: you may be able to see it but may also find that your hand passes through it without resistance. It may not be perceptible to everyone. One person may see a ghost standing in a corner of the room, but others who are present may not. Finally and perhaps most important, the existence of ghosts is highly disputed. Even if the experience satisfies all the other criteria — say there are several people present who witness the same thing — it will probably be doubted later by those who were not there (and maybe by some who were) on the grounds that there is no such thing as ghosts.

The criteria I've given seem to be more or less universal, prevailing over most if not all periods and cultures. What is accounted as real must fit into our preconceptions. I must add, however, that the *content* of our preconceptions may differ according to time and place, sometimes wildly. Many cultures today give far more credence than we do to such things as ghosts, spirits good and evil, possession, witchcraft, and similar things. So, for that matter, did Western civilization five hundred years ago. It's strange to read court testimonies from the era of the witch hunts and encounter a man who confesses to turning himself into a toad — along with a judge and jury who accept his testimony.

We can see how these criteria work by examining cases where the reality of a thing is subject to doubt. The parapsychologist Andrija Puharich tells of a study of the Indian rope trick. Long a mainstay of fakirs, the trick runs so relentlessly counter to our views of reality — and even of what sleight of hand can accomplish — that some have denied it has ever been done at all.

Puharich describes a demonstration of this trick arranged by some scientists:

> Dr. Rudolf von Urban, Dr. Alexander Pilcz, and some col-leagues made a study of the Indian Rope Trick. They were interested in the problem of mass hallucination and it was their idea that the Indian Rope Trick would serve as a good experi-ment for their purposes. They collected several hundred people and a Fakir to put on the show. They saw the Fakir throw a coil of rope in the air and saw a small boy climb up the rope and disappear. Subsequently dismembered parts of this small boy came tumbling to the ground; the Fakir gathered them up in the basket, ascended the rope, and both the boy and the Fakir came down smiling. It is astonishing that several hundred people wit-nessed this demonstration and agreed in general on the details as described. There was not a single person present in the crowd who could deny these facts. However, when the motion pic-tures of this scene were developed subsequently, it was found that the Fakir had walked into the center of the group of people and thrown the rope into the air, but that it had fallen to the ground. The Fakir and his boy assistant had stood motion-less by the rope throughout the rest of the demonstration. The rope did not stay in the air, the boy did not ascend the rope. In other words, everyone had witnessed the same hallucination. Presumably the hallucination originated with the Fakir as the agent or sender. At no time in the course of the demonstration did the Fakir tell the audience what they were going to see. The entire demonstration was carried out in silence.[15]

How does this fit with our criteria for reality? In the first case, the idea that someone might throw a rope into the air and climb up it runs contrary to our preconceptions of how the world is, so this alone would give cause for suspicion. What proved the trick to be a hallucination was the testimony of the camera, which gave a more stereoscopic view, in this case presumably because, unlike the minds of the spectators, it was not prone to suggestion.

For those who might trust in the camera, which is supposedly incapable of deceit, I might cite a phenomenon discussed on the Internet: orbs. To quote Daniel Pinchbeck, author of *2012: The Return of Quetzalcoatl*, writing on the Reality Sandwich website: "Orbs are best known as those mysterious balls of light that have appeared on digital photographs for the last fifteen years, though some claim they can see them with the naked eye as well. Orbs have spawned an enthusiastic subculture of people who believe the blobby wisps are not dust particles or lens anomalies, but angels, spirits, other-dimensional beings and so on.... Most people first discover orbs when they are trying to photograph something else — friends at a party, a politician, their cat."[16]

In this case, it would appear to be the camera that is suffering from the delusion. Again the doubt is triggered by our preconceptions: people generally don't believe there are orbs of light floating around the air. Moreover, orbs are not stable; they are evanescent; and they don't stand up very well to stereoscopic examination. Sometimes they show up on camera, sometimes they can be seen with the naked eye, but a rigorous criterion for reality would demand that they appear to *both* the camera and the naked eye and, moreover, appear in much the same way to both. A person who sees an orb, or takes a picture of one that cannot be explained as some fluke of lighting, may not be persuaded that what he saw was unreal. But someone who hears about it secondhand will probably be much more suspicious.

Set down on paper, these criteria may seem utterly obvious and pedestrian. So they should. They underpin practically every move we make. They have been established as a solid basis for enabling us to function on the plane of existence that we call the physical world. They have been hashed out over millennia of human life; no attempt at vindication on my part would validate them any further, and no attempt at refutation would weaken our reliance on them. Even so, looking at them as a whole, we might notice one startling fact: a great deal of what we experience is not "real" in this sense, including thoughts, dreams, fantasies, even ideas and concepts.

I say more about this issue in chapter 5, but to give a quick illustration of what I'm talking about, think of a green lion. Green lions don't exist; we can all agree on that. Yet you can imagine such a thing without too much difficulty. Assume also that you have some talent for cartooning. You make some sketches of this green lion, and soon you begin to draft some stories about it. You decide that they're pretty good, and you take them to a friend who works for a children's television network. The network likes the sketches and invites you to turn them into a series. Pretty soon you have made millions of dollars out of something that, as we agreed initially, doesn't exist.

Is money itself real? The overwhelming testimony of the majority of Americans suggests that it is. In the old days, people used the expression "sound as a dollar." While Americans today don't have the unshakable faith in our currency that we did a couple of generations ago, we are possibly more prone than ever to account for everything in terms of its value in dollars and cents. The bottom line is a Moloch to which everything in our lives is sacrificed. But where is this supposedly real money? It no longer takes the solid form of gold and silver; much of it no longer exists even as coins or paper currency. For the most part it consists of nothing more substantial than lines of numbers in the computers of banks and the Federal Reserve. With the great financial crash of 2008, we witnessed trillions of dollars evaporate overnight. This money existed nowhere except in the highly abstract form of putative values assigned to certain types of debt. When it was discovered or decided that there were no such values, the money evaporated and large investment houses immediately collapsed.

Hence reality, in the sense I've indicated, is only one small part of the panoply of human experience. And yet we all too often take it as the only dimension of life that is worth bothering with at all. One of the grimmest personifications of this attitude is Mr. Gradgrind, the brutally practical industrialist in Charles Dickens's novel *Hard Times*: "A man of realities. A man of fact and calculations. A man who proceeds upon the principle that two and two are four, and nothing over, and who is not to be talked into allowing for anything over.... With a rule and a pair of scales, and the multiplication table always in his pocket, sir, ready to weigh and measure any parcel of human nature, and tell you exactly what it comes to."[17] This is our civilization in sum, its industry and its economics and its science, and more and more often its philosophy and religion as well. We can look at this Gradgrindian world as it has taken shape around us and see how much we like the result.

Such is the trap the West has fallen into, but it is not the only one possible. Some more rarefied and abstract sensibilities go in the other direction. Like Plato, they say that only the eternal is truly real, and everything else is milling around "somewhere between unreality and perfect reality." This is also one meaning of a familiar prayer from the Upanishads:

From the unreal (*asat*) lead me to the real (*sat*)!
From darkness lead me to light!
From death lead me to immortality![18]

The Advaita Vedanta school of Indian philosophy expresses this attitude in its very terminology. Consciousness (what the Samkhya school calls *purusha*) it knows as Brahman or atman,

atman meaning "Self"; *prakriti* is *maya*, or illusion. According to Shankara, the great theorist of Advaita Vedanta, only what is changeless in the "three times" — past, present, and future — is real; all else is illusory. This is the version of Hindu philosophy that is best known in the West, but it is not the only one that exists. Another view, described by Sir John Woodroffe, the great scholar of Indian religion, is "that the world is Siva's Experience and Siva's Experience can never be unreal."[19] (I say more about the relation between the Samkhya and the Advaita Vedanta in the next chapter.)

Certainly it would be quixotic to launch a crusade to change the meaning of the term *real* as it is used in our civilization. But we need not be enslaved by words. Simply by acknowledging that experience extends far beyond material substance, we can step out into new dimensions of life and mind, as the esoteric traditions have always called us to do. Trees and stones and human artifacts have solidity and obey certain laws of physics; but in their own realms, so do dreams and imaginings and our occasional glimpses of transcendent being. Shiva and Parvati play the game of consciousness on more boards than one.

CHAPTER THREE

TWO AGAINST ONE
The Persistence of Dualism

When Parvati, in the guise of the bewitching untouchable, tries to coax Shiva back into her embrace, she remarks that he is an ascetic living free from duality. What exactly does she mean by this? And why should duality be a good thing to avoid?

The number two is widely regarded as an ill omen. Because two is the first number to break away from unity, it is the number of the devil, and forked or two-pronged objects are frequently associated with him. Indeed *deuce* is often a euphemism for the devil. Jewish and Christian mystics noted that in Genesis the second day of creation was the only one that God did not pronounce good, and the unclean beasts went two by two into Noah's ark, while the clean ones entered by sevens.[1] And in craps, the two, or "snake eyes," is a losing throw.

This unfortunate number has proved no more auspicious for the philosophical systems associated with it. The term *dualism* has been applied to several different theories in different fields, all of them generally discredited. In the philosophy of mind, it refers to

41

René Descartes's view that the mind and the body are two utterly separate and distinct entities, running on parallel courses and connected only at the pineal gland in the center of the head. Descartes had his own ingenious reasons for making this claim: for example, the fact that I can imagine myself without a body, but I cannot imagine myself without a mind, since the very fact of imagining *means* that I have a mind. Nevertheless, few philosophers have accepted Descartes's view, partly because it seems to do little justice to the exquisite interaction between body and mind. If the two are so separate, why should the one affect the other at all? Yet as we all know, when the body drinks, the mind gets drunk.[2]

Originally, the word *dualism* was not meant to refer to Descartes's philosophy. It was coined around 1700 to characterize certain religious teachings which held that the world is produced by the contention of two more or less equal forces, the good and the evil, or the light and the dark. In the purest dualistic systems, such as Manichaeism, these two forces are fundamentally irreconcilable: they do not spring from the same source and can never be harmonized. The ultimate redemption of the universe comes, not from integrating the two or even destroying the evil, but from an elaborate form of cosmic purification in which the hidden particles of light are filtered out from the darkness of matter that ensnares them.

Manichaeism, named after its founder, a prophet named Mani who lived in Mesopotamia in the fourth century AD, flourished for almost a thousand years in regions from China to North Africa. It probably (this claim is controversial) gave rise to the medieval heresies of Bogomilism and Catharism. But Manichaeism and its heirs failed to catch on in the long run. The reasons are complex — for one thing, these movements were severely persecuted by their rivals — but had a great deal to do with their gloomy exclusivism and their belief that the manifest world was irredeemably evil. By approximately 1400, they were for all purposes extinct.[3]

Dualistic religion may have been easy to eradicate, but dualistic thinking is not so easily avoided. My late friend Dr. Frederic Spiegelberg, emeritus professor of religion at Stanford University, was fond of saying that most people are Manichaeans without knowing it, making rigid and categorical distinctions between good and evil, us and them, and so on. The Russian philosopher P. D. Ouspensky makes a similar observation about the "formatory center," which is his name for the mechanical aspect of the intellect: "The formatory center can only count up to two. It always divides everything in two: 'bolshevism and fascism,' 'workers and bourgeois,' 'proletarians and capitalists,' and so on. We owe most modern catchwords to formatory thinking, and not only catchwords but all modern popular theories. Perhaps it is possible to say that at all times all popular theories are formatory."[4] More recently, psychologist Stephen Larsen has pointed out that this kind of either-or thinking is prompted and enhanced by irrational fear: "If you wish to induce a state of compliance in your would-be constituency, it is clearly an advantage to frighten them. First induce the . . . fear response, and then offer them a loaded choice: be saved or be damned; convert or die." Larsen links the worldwide epidemic of fanatical fundamentalism to this habit of mind.[5]

Then there is theological dualism: the belief in a creation that is radically *other* than its creator, so that the gulf between God and his creatures can never be crossed. Christianity in its most common forms is dualistic in this sense. Here is a more or less typical statement of the prevailing view, in the words of the Presbyterian moderator of the Soc.religion.christian newsgroup: "Christianity conceives of God as One. But it is not an isolated One. Rather, God is a person, who is capable of affecting and being affected by others.... In contrast to pantheist and related concepts, the creation is genuinely distinct from God. The world has a genuine existence of its own. God cares about and interacts with the creation. Human beings are responsible to God. As the creator, God is responsible for the world and its history. While ... the world is distinct from God, it is not completely independent. God is thought of as continuously sustaining the world."[6] Contrast the foregoing with this view, stated on the website of the Florida-based Center for Non-Dualism: "Non-Dualism is the orientation that there is one absolute reality without a second, and that each of us, although an individual person, is one with that reality, just as a wave is not separate from the ocean."[7] Most Christian theologians would find it hard to agree with this statement.

Even attempts to transcend dualism often end up doing unwitting obeisance to it. In his book *The Coming of the Cosmic Christ*, the renegade Dominican monk Matthew Fox lashes out in denunciation of dualistic thinking: "War is by definition anthropocentric dualism carried to its logical conclusion: I kill you; you kill me; we kill them; they kill us." But in order to save us from this mentality, he gives a list of things we must move away *from* and *toward* — all set out in a helpful two-column format.[8] What could be more dualistic than that?

These types of dualism are not my focus here, but I've mentioned them because, while dualism is frequently attacked, it is not always clear which form is the target. The type of dualism that I discuss here is the sort typified by the Samkhya and certain other forms of traditional philosophy. I bring attention to it not out of some arcane interest in obscure Eastern systems but because it touches profoundly on our notions of — and experience of — reality.

First, however, it's probably necessary to say something about the Samkhya. It is considered to be one of six "orthodox" *darshans*, or perspectives, on the Hindu sacred texts known as the Vedas. Of the other five, one, Yoga, is a household word in the United States, but the traditional Yoga is not an array of stretching exercises; it is a rigorous system of meditative practice that is meant to confer *moksha*, or spiritual liberation. Another of the six *darshans*, Vedanta, is well known to students of Eastern philosophy (I will say more about it later); the other three, Mimamsa, Nyaya, and Vaisheshika, are recondite schools dealing mostly with logic and cosmology and are all but unknown here.

Samkhya in Sanskrit means something like "enumeration" but might be better rendered as "analysis." It is a system that analyzes reality into its fundamental components, not for the sake of mere speculation, but as a means of spiritual liberation. Although I've just said that the Samkhya and Yoga are two separate perspectives on the Hindu sacred tradition, this was not always the case. Heinrich Zimmer, the great scholar of Indian religion, points out, "These two are regarded in India as twins, the two aspects of a single discipline." He comments:

> As we read in the *Bhagavad Gita*: "Puerile and unlearned people speak of 'enumerating knowledge' (*sankhya*) and the 'practice of introvert concentration' (*yoga*) as distinct from each other, yet anyone firmly established in either gains the fruit of both. The state attained by the followers of the path of enumerating knowledge is attained also through the exercises of introvert concentration. He truly sees who regards as one the intellectual attitude of enumerating knowledge and the practice of concentration." The two systems, in other words, supplement each other and conduce to the same goal.[9]

Originally, then, the Samkhya was regarded as the theory and Yoga as the practice. It's particularly striking to realize that the

Sanskrit root of yoga is *yunakti*, "to yoke" (cognate with our own word *yoke*). If we render the word as *integration*, the two perspectives together are defined as "analysis" and "integration" and are revealed to be complements of each other. Something must be broken down and something else integrated, rather as in the old alchemical formula "Solve et coagula": "Dissolve and coagulate."

The origins of the Samkhya are lost in the remote past. Traditionally its founder was held to be one Kapila, a sage about whom nothing is known. He is sometimes identified with a monk of that name in the Indian epic cycle, who slew the sixty thousand warrior sons of a king with one glance. (The nineteenth-century esotericist H. P. Blavatsky explains the myth: "The 60,000 *Sons*, brutal, vicious, and impious, are the personification of the *human passions* that 'a mere glance of the sage' — the Self who represents the highest stage of purity that can be reached on earth — reduces to ashes.")[10]

In any event, the first ideas resembling those of the Samkhya can be found in the Katha Upanishad, dated to as early as the fourth century BCE, and, as we've just seen, in the Bhagavad Gita, dated roughly to between 500 and 200 BC.[11] The period of the classical Samkhya, however, is AD 300–600; its crowning text is the *Samkhyakarika* of Ishvarakrishna, which must have been well known by AD 560, as it was translated into Chinese around that date.[12]

Whether the Samkhya still survives as a living philosophical tradition in India is unclear. A couple of years ago I asked this question of a Hindu scholar with whom I happened to be chatting; he told me that it did not survive, that it had been absorbed by other philosophical schools, particularly the Vedanta. The scholar K. B. Ramakrishna Rao, writing in the 1960s, asserted, "The Samkhya is an out-moded [school of] thought now.... If at any time Samkhya is mentioned, it is only as an adversary.... It has only a historical value and its influence as a philosophy has practically disappeared."[13]

But this may not be entirely the case. Gerald J. Larson, perhaps the foremost scholar of the Samkhya in the West, writes, "I had been under the impression that Samkhya was no longer a living tradition in India," but then he discovered a monastery by the name of Kapila Matha in the Indian state of Bihar that claimed to be practicing Samkhyayoga.[14] Probably the best-known presentation of the Samkhya in the West is in *To Live Within*, a highly regarded memoir by Lizelle Reymond about her studies in a Himalayan hermitage with the Samkhya master Sri Anirvan (1896–1978) in the middle of the twentieth century.[15]

Living or defunct, the Samkhya, as I've said, is a philosophical teaching that is meant to confer spiritual liberation. What is it liberation *from?*

From the conventional, limited, and delusory view of reality. This view is represented in every transitive sentence. There is a subject and an object — two separate things — linked by an action represented by a verb:

$$\text{Subject} \rightarrow \text{Verb} \rightarrow \text{Object}$$

This stance is so apparently rock-solid that it can be difficult to shake oneself free from it. Meditation in its many forms is one way of doing so, but there are others, including, of course, spontaneous insight.

To taste the experience of liberation, simply close your eyes while remaining alert. Watch the thoughts flicker across the screen of your mind like images on a film. At first you may feel attachment or aversion to some of these images. They are emphatically "mine" or "not mine": that is, they are accepted or rejected depending on any number of factors. But if you can begin to relax these automatic responses, you can watch these impressions more impartially, neither clinging to them nor pushing them away. You realize that they come and go on their own; there is not much you can do to stop them. At the same time, this very realization opens up a certain amount of space between you and these thoughts, no matter how intensely you ordinarily identify with them. You recognize that they are not you. You begin to intuit the fact that you are actually the silent, nameless, qualityless watcher that observes all these things. Your experience begins to take this shape:

Watcher → Impressions

The "watcher" is what the Samkhya calls *purusha*. Here is how the *Samkhyakarika* characterizes *purusha*: It is "(a) a witness; (b) possessed of isolation or freedom; (c) indifferent; (d) a spectator; (e) and inactive." The stream of impressions is *prakriti*. It is not conscious, but "because of the proximity (or association) of the two — i.e., *prakriti* and *purusa* — the unconscious one appears as if characterized by consciousness."[16]

To glimpse this truth — that what is conscious in us is distinct from what it experiences, even internally — gives a profound insight into human nature and destiny. As Larson writes, "Man's deepest selfhood, according to classical Samkhya, is not his empirical ego structure or even his intelligence. Man's deepest selfhood is rather the very fact of consciousness."[17]

The relationship between *purusha* and *prakriti*, between consciousness and its experience, is subtle. Indeed the disputes on this point mark some of the principal differences among the various Hindu schools of philosophy and between these schools and Buddhism. It's important to touch on some of these differences because of the light they cast on the nature of mind.

To begin with, as we've already seen, *prakriti* is not conscious. Why? Because it is by definition that which *is seen* — it is in its entirety the contents of consciousness. But as noted in the quoted text, because of the presence of *purusha* "the unconscious one appears as if characterized by consciousness." *Prakriti* acquires a kind of fictitious consciousness because *purusha* is identified with it. (Or as the myth puts it, Parvati cheats Shiva out of his attributes.) As paradoxical as this may sound, it is nothing more than you can see with even a little meditative experience. Usually you believe that the stream of thoughts and feelings that course through your mind are you; you identify with them. But if you step back and look at them, you can see that they are not you. Actually the very fact that you can see them from a distance proves that they are not you. What *is* you is the silent witness that is ever present, ever seeing, and ever still.

Prakriti, by contrast, is unconscious but perpetually active. It is the source of all the movement, energy, and dynamism of the universe. As you know, you can't stop the movement of the universe for a single second. In fact you can barely stop the movement of your own thoughts for a single second. This is the power of *prakriti*. In Hindu philosophy, this power has a name of its own: *shakti*, the primal energy that animates all things. The occult philosophers of the European Renaissance had a similar concept: they called it *anima mundi*, "the soul of the world." *Shakti* is the source and substance of the endless *doing* that constitutes so much of our lives and indeed of the universe.

The Samkhya does not speak of *shakti* as such. Rather it divides the action of *prakriti* into three *gunas*, or "strands." One is *rajas*, the source of all movement. The second is *tamas*: inertia. The third is *sattva*, the force of balance and equilibration. Everything in manifest existence is made up of these three forces in varying degrees of admixture.[18]

It is not hard to see in the *gunas* the sacred ternary that undergirds many esoteric traditions. Gurdjieff spoke of three forces, which he called "Holy Affirming," "Holy Denying," and "Holy Reconciling." These can be related to *rajas*, *tamas*, and *sattva*, respectively. So can the traditional Chinese trinity of Heaven above, Earth beneath, and Man, the entity that connects the two. Even the Christian Trinity resembles this schema, with the ever-begetting Father, the ever-begotten Son, and the Holy Spirit, the Comforter or reconciler. Nor should this surprise us: if these truths are universal, they must have been discovered and known universally, no matter about the differences in names and nuances.

The next phase of insight is more difficult. It requires you to see not only your thoughts but your own actions, and your impulses toward action, as external to the Self. Now it is not so much "I want to move," but rather "the impulse to move arises." This impulse arises out of *prakriti*. Action may well follow: you get up. But here too the entirety of the action — the impulse toward movement, as well as the action itself — can be revealed as nothing more than a collection of impressions. The silent watcher does not "do" them; rather it watches these impulses, the activity of the *gunas*, arise and cohere and dissolve; it is, as the *Samkhyakarika* says, "inactive."

The watcher, then, turns out to be rather passive. It has been characterized that way by other traditions as well. Esoteric Christianity — which is not so far from the Samkhya as one might think — frequently speaks of "passions." These are not the same as the passions that we ordinarily think of when we consider the term; probably the best word for them in present-day English is *impulses*, which has something of the impersonal and quasi-external connotation that is necessary. Our word *passion* is derived from the Latin *pati*, "to suffer"; it has the same root as *passive*, as is obvious on the printed page. Passions are not something that consciousness does; rather they are something it experiences, it *suffers* in every sense of that word.*

In the Samkhya, the whole process of spiritual liberation is *kaivalya*, or "isolation" — the detachment of *purusha*, or primordial mind, from its experience.[19] You are not your thoughts; you are not your feelings; you are not even your actions. This realization in expressed in the myth of the dice game: Shiva, having "lost" all his attributes to Parvati, goes off, unruffled, to the forest to live the life of an ascetic. *Purusha* has no attributes; they all belong to *prakriti*; that is why *purusha* always loses the game. But since these attributes are not part of it to begin with, it loses nothing in actuality. Here is how the *Samkhyakarika* characterizes this state:

> Then, the *purusa*, comfortably situated like a spectator, sees *prakriti* whose activity has ceased due to the completion of her purpose, and who has turned back from the seven forms. . . .
>
> (Says the) indifferent one (or spectator), "I have seen (her)"; the other ceases saying, "I have been seen." Though the two are still in proximity, no (further) creation (takes place).[20]

Although in this passage *purusha* is "comfortably seated like a spectator," the ultimate Samkhya goal of isolation, the utter and irreversible divorce of consciousness from all of its experience, does not offer an attractive prospect to the Western sensibility or, possibly, to any sensibility. In fact the Samkhya may have gone into eclipse partly for this reason. "The description of the state of salvation as *kaivalya* ('isolation') is a stark, austere mode

---

* Esoteric Christianity does not, of course, use the word *purusha*. Its equivalent in Greek, the language in which esoteric Christianity was formulated, is *nous*, sometimes translated as "consciousness" or mistranslated as "intellect." The Greek equivalent for passions, *pathē*, has an etymology and connotation similar to those of the English and Latin words.

of religious thought, which obviously would exercise little popular appeal," as Larson observes.[21]

There are other likely reasons for the decline of the Samkhya. Some are of little concern here: political instability in India in the late first millennium AD; the increasing ossification of the Samkhya into a standardized system that allowed little room for original thought; and its reluctance to generate religious institutions.[22] But this stark and nihilistic picture of salvation must have been one of the most crucial factors. To many, the Samkhya goal of *kaivalya* must have looked as dispiriting as agnostic materialism did to me at Oxford.

Another element in the Samkhya's decline may have been its teaching that there are many *purushas*. That is to say, there is not one great consciousness in which all partake but any number of atomized bits of consciousness that can only be liberated and sent into ultimate isolation. This too was no doubt dispiriting. Moreover, the reasons posited for it in the Samkhya are not convincing:

> The plurality of *purusas* is established,
>
> (a) because of the diversity of births, deaths, and faculties;
>
> (b) because of actions or functions (that take place) at different times;
>
> (c) and because of differences in the proportions of the three *gunas* (in different entities).[23]

This argument is easily refuted. If, as the Samkhya says, *purusha* and *prakriti* are radically and ultimately distinct and have nothing to do with one another, how could all these actions, functions, births, deaths, *gunas*, and so on have anything genuine to do with *purusha*? They too are elements of *prakriti*. Therefore the concept of the plurality of *purushas* collapses, and we are left with one, single, indivisible *purusha*, one universal consciousness that, because of its mistaken self-identification with the doings of *prakriti*, imagines itself to be plural.

The Vedas, the sacred scriptures from which all orthodox Hindu systems claim their authority, portray *purusha* as Man, the cosmic human, or, in the words of Heinrich Zimmer, "the living entity behind and within all the metamorphoses of our life in bondage."[24] A Vedic hymn says:

> The Man [literally *purusha*] as a thousand heads, a thousand eyes, a thousand feet. He pervaded the earth on all sides and extended beyond it as far as ten fingers.
>
> It is the Man who is all this, whatever has been and whatever is to be. He is the ruler of immortality. . . .
>
> Such is his greatness, and the Man is yet more than that. All creatures are a quarter of him; three quarters of him are what is immortal in heaven.[25]

Purusha is not a familiar term even among many Westerners who are interested in Hindu philosophy. A more common word is *atman*, often rendered as "Self" (usually capitalized). This usage comes from the Advaita Vedanta, which is by far the best known of all Hindu philosophies in the West, largely because many of the most illustrious Hindu mystics of the past century and a half — such as Sri Ramakrishna, Swami Vivekananda, and Sri Ramana Maharshi — belonged to this school. *Advaita* means "nondual." (There are dualistic and semidualistic forms of Vedanta, but they are almost unknown in the West.)[26] Unlike the Samkhya, Advaita Vedanta teaches that mind consists not of an infinite number of atomistic *purushas* but of one single atman. Moreover, atman is Brahman, the supreme creator. There is no dualism — that is, there is ultimately no distinction between the Self that lies embedded in each of us (located in the heart and no bigger than a thumb, according to one of the Upanishads)[27] and the creator of the universe.

This view, taken to its logical conclusion, overturns even some of the doctrines often associated with Hinduism. My friend Dr. Spiegelberg once told me of a conversation he had with Ananda K. Coomaraswamy, the great scholar of Indian religion. Dr. Spiegelberg asked Coomaraswamy if he believed in reincarnation. Coomaraswamy said nothing for a painfully long time — perhaps five minutes. Finally he replied, "No. It is all Brahman. It is all one." To Coomaraswamy, even the concept of an individual self that reincarnates was, in an ultimate sense, false. All beings are mere manifestations of Brahman, the creator and soul of the universe. This may not be much consolation to those who want to be assured of personal survival, but then it is saying that personal survival is not necessary. Personal survival is ultimately only an obstruction to the knowledge of the immortal and indestructible Self.

Illusion, *maya* in Sanskrit, plays a crucial role in Advaita Vedanta, for reasons that may already be plain. If everything is actually one, where does the multiplicity of things come from? Multiplicity can't be so in fact; it must be merely appearance. Hence the manifest universe is illusory — but not in the way we customarily understand that word. To us, a mirage is an illusion; it is an image of something that is not there. *Maya* to the Vedantins is different. As Hans Torwesten explains in his introduction to the Vedanta philosophy:

> Where this maya-mirage obtains — and for most people it is very much *there* — it is not only taken for real but also for the totality of reality. Yet the moment enlightenment occurs the whole mirage vanishes in a flash. The comparison with someone waking from a dream is obvious. We may laugh about it afterward. Over and over in Vedanta literature we find

enlightenment and illusion compared to a rope taken for a snake in insufficient light. For the person experiencing this, the illusionary snake is very real indeed — but in bright light the imagined snake is instantly revealed to be just a rope.[28]

The rope-snake analogy resembles the incident mentioned in chapter 2 in which I mistook a crumpled piece of tissue for a mouse. But the thrust of the Vedanta metaphor is different: Everything we see is like a rope mistaken for a snake. We misunderstand the fundamental nature of everything. As Coomaraswamy says, "It is all Brahman. It is all one."

In this discussion we must avoid the semantic trap hidden in the words *real* and *reality*. As I've already pointed out, in English these words are very closely tied to thingness. To say a thing is unreal, then, is very much like saying a thing is not a thing: an obvious contradiction. The Vedanta does not say that. Rather, it says we fail to recognize that all things are manifestations of the One. In the words of Shankara, the greatest exponent of the Advaita Vedanta, "Man drinks the wine of Maya, becomes deluded and begins to see things as separate from each other, so that he talks of 'you' and 'I.'"[29] Perceiving the world as a series of separate, isolated entities is *maya*, and realizing the truth is enlightenment. Shankara also writes, "All the things which we perceive exist here within (in our Self . . .). Within is the whole of this universe. By Maya it appears as external, like one's own body in a mirror."[30]

In his most renowned work, *The Crest-Jewel of Discrimination*, Shankara discourses on the nature of *maya*:

> She has no beginning. She is composed of the three gunas, subtle, beyond perception. It is from the effects she produces that her existence is inferred by the wise. It is she who gives birth to the whole universe.
>
> She is neither being nor non-being, nor a mixture of both.

She is neither divided nor undivided, nor a mixture of both. She is neither an indivisible whole, nor composed of parts, nor a mixture of both. She is most strange. Her nature is inexplicable.[31]

There is another sense in which the Vedanta contends that the world is illusory: when you awaken from it, the world ceases to exist. Another classic Advaita text, the *Yoga Vasistha*, says, "As soon as we come to know our true nature (the Supreme Reality), all sensations, perceptions and conceptions . . . wither away. With the direct knowledge of the Supreme Reality, we directly cognise their absence."[32]

Although Shankara took great pains to refute the Samkhya philosophy, the difference between the Samkhya and his Advaita Vedanta are comparatively small and subtle. As the Vedantin Swami Prabhavananda has observed, the "concept of Prakriti corresponds, more or less, to Shankara's concept of Maya — but with this important difference: Prakriti is said to be other than, and independent of[,] Purusha (the absolute Reality) while Maya is said to have no absolute reality but to be dependent on Brahman."[33]

This makes sense as far as it goes, at least if we interpret it to mean that there can be no experience (*maya* or *prakriti*) without an experiencer (Brahman or atman in the Vedanta, *purusha* in the Samkhya). All the same, much of the Advaita Vedanta is frustrating Like many nondualistic views, it stumbles at this question: if everything is Brahman and Brahman is all-knowing — indeed Brahman *is* knowing — how did this delusion known as *maya* come to exist in the first place? How did pure knowing give rise to not-knowing?

The Vedanta's answer is more than a little vague. Shankara writes, "The sun's rays bring forth layers of cloud. By them, the sun is concealed; and so it appears that the clouds alone exist. In the same way, the ego, which is brought forth by the Atman, hides the true nature of the Atman; and so it appears that the ego alone exists."[34] Swami Prabhavananda adds, "We are forced to conclude, as Shankara does, that Maya, like Brahman, is without any beginning. Ignorance as the cause and world-appearance as the effect have existed always and will always exist. They are like seed and tree. The 'coupling of the real and unreal,' produced by our ignorance, is a process universally evident in our daily lives."[35] But none of this really tells how or why the ego is "brought forth by the Atman" — that is, how not-knowing can be produced by pure knowing.

Moreover, if all is Brahman, all is one, then we might expect the Advaita Vedanta to espouse a version of what some Christian theologians call the *via positiva*, or "positive way" — in this context, a total identification of all things with Brahman, since all things *are* Brahman. The Vedanta's mystical techniques would involve ecstatic union rather than radical detachment, which one might identify with dualistic philosophies such as the Samkhya.

But the thrust of Advaita Vedanta is quite the opposite. Constantly it preaches detachment. To the question "Who is free?" Shankara replies, "He who is dispassionate." Elsewhere he says:

> Kill this deadly attachment to body, wife, children and others. The seers who have overcome it go to that high dwelling-place of Vishnu, the all-pervading.
>
> This body, which is made up of skin, flesh, blood, arteries, veins, fat, marrow and bone, is full of waste matter and filth. It deserves our contempt.[36]

Hardly a prescription for ecstatic union. This peculiar emphasis on the ultimate unity of all things, combined with a remorseless urge to detachment, helps explain why Sri Anirvan could say, "Modern India . . . follows intellectually a philosophical religion which is composed for the most part of *Samkhya* with a little

Vedanta. Every cultured person knows it."[37] Although Sri Anirvan was a Samkhya master, I suspect that this judgment was more than just special pleading.

To go any further into these issues would take us deeper into the thickets of Indian philosophy than would be useful here, so let's step back and take stock of what we've surveyed.

In the first place, dualism is not so easy to avoid. There seems to remain the fundamental distinction between consciousness and its contents — that which *sees* and that which *is seen*, at all levels and in all dimensions. That which is seen is by definition unconscious. Hence the Samkhya's emphasis on the blind nature of *prakriti*. Moreover, *purusha*, consciousness, has no characteristics other than pure cognition. Strictly understood, it is neither infinite nor finite, neither individual nor collective. It can assume any or all of these features or none. That is why the Samkhya sees it as particular and the Vedanta as collective.

Purusha is both devoid of characteristics and endlessly mutable. All possibilities are open to it — including being bound to its own experience and confusing itself with what it experiences. It can become, or seem to become, what it beholds. This is one meaning of the Greek myth of Narcissus, who drowns while admiring his own reflection in the water. Consciousness "drowns" in this way. As paradoxical as this may sound, it loses consciousness by being identified with its own reflections, its own experience. This is the meaning of *maya* or, to use another Sanskrit term, *avidya* — "ignorance" or, more accurately, "obliviousness."

For consciousness to lose consciousness is, of course, a contradiction in terms (which also may help explain why the Vedanta regards it as illusory). But in the world as we know it, this situation happens often and, for practically the entire human race, inevitably. Some kind of liberation is necessary, whether we call it enlightenment, illumination, "isolation," gnosis, or some other name. This liberation necessarily requires the detachment of consciousness from its contents, in a way suggested by the exercise I sketched earlier. Regardless of what one experiences, one needs to detach the Self from what it mistakenly believes itself to be. In the language of the myth, no matter how the dice are thrown, Shiva loses to Parvati. He *must* lose. Everything he takes himself to be in fact belongs to her.

The result of this loss is, surprisingly, bliss. Shiva goes off contentedly to live the life of a forest ascetic. This is the stage that the Samkhya equates with "isolation." It is not a stark, barren, nihilistic kind of isolation of the sort experienced by the heroes of existentialist novels, but the bliss of perfect freedom and equanimity. You can encounter it at times in meditation, which can produce a state of *samadhi* — a kind of consciousness without contents that is both peaceful and blissful.

Even this phase is not the complete story. Parvati goes off in search of Shiva again, and eventually they reunite. That is, after detaching itself from its experience, consciousness reunites with it, but this time in a lighter, more balanced fashion. *Purusha* is no longer, like Narcissus, submerged in *prakriti*. As noted earlier, the *Samkhyakarika* puts it this way: "Though the two are still in proximity, no (further) creation (takes place)." Consciousness is aware of all it experiences — thoughts, feelings, even passions come and go — but is not enslaved by these things, does not cling to or identify itself with them.

We could go through the myths and scriptures of many traditions and find countless expressions of these truths. In Egyptian myth, Osiris — the personification of what the Hindus call *purusha* — is slain and cut into pieces by his brother Set, who represents the force of oblivion.[38] Osiris's wife, Isis, the force of awakening, collects the scattered pieces of his corpse and reassembles and restores life to them. In short, consciousness is dismembered by its own attachment to and identification with multiplicity. Esoterically understood, this is death. The esoteric meaning of the story of Christ is much the same. The God-man descends to earth; he is crucified on a cross of time and space, but he rises again on the third day to new life. Consciousness takes form in the world, where it is crucified by the vicissitudes of its own experience, but in the end it does not matter. Because it is immortal and indestructible, even its apparent death is unimportant, as it will rise from the dead in a new and more glorious form. The similarity of these and many other death-and-resurrection myths indicates that this truth, perhaps the central one of human life, has been universally recognized and handed down over millennia.

The myths may explain how this all happens, but they are considerably less explicit about why. Why should it be like this, and not some other way? The Kabbalah says that the universe was created so that God could behold God in his own reflection. Of course, insofar as this reflection is *seen*, insofar as it is the object of knowledge, it cannot at the same time and in the same way be the subject. That is, knowing must of necessity bring about not-knowing. As I emphasized in chapter 2, there is no absolute stance of knowing or not-knowing; the knower is, or can be, known. But insofar as it has the aspect of the known — and everything in the manifest world has this aspect to some degree — it is mindless and unseeing. This is the source of the *maya* and the *avidya* of which the Indian philosophers speak. It is also the *samsara*, "delusion," of the Buddhists. A text attributed to Padmasambhava, the legendary wizard who brought Buddhism to Tibet in the eighth century AD, reads, "Realize that sentient beings, from the moment *they are experienced*, do not possess any true existence and therefore that samsara is the primordial purity of nonarising."[39] *Prakriti, maya, samsara* — which are essentially different words for the same thing — are built into the framework of the universe as we know it, and the universe can hardly be imagined without them. They are also built into each molecule and atom and quark of our own being.

CHAPTER FOUR

CONSTANT CONJUNCTION
The Problem of Causation

There is one philosophical problem that surpasses all others in difficulty. At the same time it's so important that it can make even the nature of being and the existence of God look like mere side issues.

I'm speaking of <u>causation</u> — the idea that certain events have certain verifiable and repeatable effects, and that these constitute the bedrock of reality. Plato summed up this concept: "Everything that becomes or is created must of necessity be created by some cause, for without a cause nothing can be created."[1]

As we saw in chapter 1, God or the gods have often been invoked to serve as causes of phenomena that people did not otherwise understand. As the philosopher Henri Frankfort says of the worldview of ancient Egypt and Mesopotamia, "The gods as personifications of power among other things fulfil early man's need for causes to explain the phenomenal world."[2] Later, philosophers such as Aristotle posited God as a First Cause on these grounds: since everything seems to have a cause that has preceded it, and since the chain of cause and effect cannot extend back forever, there must have been, as Aristotle puts it, "some prime mover, whether singular or plural, that is eternal and not itself movable."[3] God has usually been cast in this role.

Invoking God as the cause of the world in this way presupposes the existence of cause and effect as we normally understand them. At first there doesn't appear to be a problem with this: the relationship of cause and effect looks like the most rudimentary common sense. But in fact commonsense views of causation are, as philosophers have long known, extremely difficult to justify or even comprehend. As far back as 1913, the British philosopher Bertrand Russell wrote, "The law of causality, I believe, like much that passes muster among philosophers, is a relic of a bygone age, surviving, like the monarchy, only because it is erroneously supposed to do no harm."[4]

The first complete investigation of the subject goes back to Aristotle. He described four causes, all of which, he said, provide possible answers to the question of why a thing should be as it is. For a statue of Apollo, for example, you could say, "This is marble." This is the *material cause*; the nature of the matter dictates in part why a thing should be as it is. You could also say of the statue, "This was made by Phidias," Phidias being the sculptor who actually made it. This is the *efficient cause*. Another response would be: "This was made to be put in the Temple of Apollo," which would explain the purpose of its existence. This is the *final cause*. Finally, you could say, "This is Apollo," which would explain why it has the shape it has. This is the *formal cause*.[5]

Practically every modern person who reads Aristotle's account has the same response: Most of these things are not causes in any sense in which we would understand that term. The marble *caused* the statue? The form of Apollo *caused* the statue? In fact the efficient cause is the only one that we would acknowledge today as a cause in the familiar sense.

The Greek word that Aristotle used was *aitía*, and while *cause* is the best one-word equivalent for it in general (our word comes from the Latin *causa*, which was used by the medieval Scholastic philosophers to expound Aristotle's four causes), it is not, perhaps, the best translation for *aitía* here. A more idiomatic rendition would be "reason": the *reasons* that this statue is as it is include its material, its shape, its purpose, and its creator.[6] ("Reason" in this sense does not necessarily imply conscious purpose.) This helps us get closer to what Aristotle was trying to say.

In any case, one of Aristotle's four causes has been rigorously excluded from the concept of causation in current physics and biology: the final cause. Science, particularly in the past few generations, has obstinately insisted that there is no purpose in the universe or in any part of it; all things are simply the mindless and mechanical results of previous circumstances. Why has science taken this tack? Because to acknowledge a purpose is tantamount to acknowledging some sort of being who would have that purpose. This comes too close to the notion of God for science to accept.

Nevertheless, as we've seen in chapter 1, the concept of purpose, particularly in living organisms, is hard to exclude entirely. It's difficult, for example, to accept that you simply *happen* to have a hand and that it *happens* to be useful for grasping and making things. Purpose finds its way in as part of an explanation, whether that purpose belongs to the Almighty Creator or to those humble bits of goo known as DNA.

As science took shape in the seventeenth century and began to exclude the final cause from its worldview, it had to find a substitute. That substitute was determinism. The contemporary

Dutch philosopher Menno Hulswit writes, "Probably the most radical change in the meaning of cause happened during the seventeenth century, in which there emerged a strong tendency to understand causal relations as instances of deterministic laws. Causes were no longer seen as the active initiators of a change, but as inactive nodes in a law-like implication chain."[7] According to this view, something causes something else to happen as a result of certain invariable natural laws. The laws of thermodynamics are among the best-known examples.

This determinism was challenged in what may be the most influential discussion of causation since Aristotle. It appears in *A Treatise of Human Nature*, published in 1739–40 by the Scottish philosopher David Hume. Hume begins by saying that, as he looks over the whole range of things that are called causes, he can find no one characteristic they have in common. There are millions of things that are causes, but there is no one quality that all of them share; being a cause is not a property like color or size or shape. Similarly with effects.[8] He then goes on to say that cause and effect must therefore involve a relation. Its nature is this:

> We remember to have had frequent instances of the existence of one species of objects; and also remember, that the individuals of another species of objects have always attended them, and have existed in a regular order of contiguity and succession with regard to them. Thus we remember to have seen that species of object we call *flame*, and to have felt that species of sensation we call *heat*. Without any farther ceremony, we call the one cause and the other effect, and infer the existence of the one from that of the other. . . .
>
> Thus in advancing we have insensibly discover'd a new relation betwixt cause and effect. . . . This relation is their CONSTANT CONJUNCTION.[9]

Causation, then, consists of nothing but "contiguity," "succession," and "constant conjunction." One event follows another; it must follow close on; and this sequence must occur several times, more or less invariably.

Philosophers have objected to Hume's argument by contending, for example, that not every cause immediately precedes its effect, and that we sometimes infer cause-and-effect relationships from one occurrence rather than many. Such objections are legitimate but not fatal, and Hume's theory can be refined in order to cope with them. The human mind is sophisticated enough to infer, for example, that smoking is "constantly conjoined" with lung cancer even though you never see a person smoking a cigarette and then immediately coming down with cancer. Our entire sense of causation does seem to come from this "constant conjunction," even if cause and effect are separated by other things and events between. Consider this string of digits:

53535353535//2439209821529398799585354735053…

If you look at this string only up to the point of the double slashes (//), you may decide that, in this string, 3 always comes immediately after 5. You would be surprised to find that 2 was the first digit to come after the slashes. If you read the string all the way across, you would come to the more accurate view that 3 always appears as the third digit after 5, hence: **5**29**3**…**5**85**3**…and so on. This holds true no matter what two numbers fall between. Using this reasoning, you don't know what the first number will be if this string of digits continues past the ellipsis (…), but you *do* know that the next one after that will be a 3, because there was a 5 three digits before.

The mind is clever enough to recognize patterns like this as well as ones that are far more complicated. What if you had volumes and volumes of these strings to analyze, and it were the case that this 5-3 sequence stopped after a certain point, only to resume exactly one thousand digits later? Could you keep the digits straight enough in your head so that you could discern this pattern? Probably not without a great deal of effort (today this kind of task would be relegated to a computer), although it would still be possible. Now imagine whether you would be able to do this if it were not merely an abstract exercise but offered some real and palpable benefit to you. Say that your recognition of this kind of pattern enabled you to find food or avoid a predator. Say furthermore that this is all your mind has to do, and that it was trained to do this and practically nothing else since you were born. You would probably find that you are able to recognize even very intricate patterns with very long intervals between them. And isn't that what the senses are trained to do? Our system of vision is not built to recognize digits primarily, but it is capable of detecting far more elaborate patterns and sequences in the patches of light and color that the eyes transmit to the brain.

It would seem, however, that this sense of cause and effect involves something more than mere contiguity in time and space. Hume also says that a cause is "an object followed by another, and whose appearance always conveys the thought to that other."[10] It's this process of association that, according to Hume, creates an impression of the necessary connection in our sense of causality. Strictly speaking, the strings of events and things in the world, like the digits set out earlier, do not *cause* each other. We simply see similarities of pattern; the mind through its own processing turns this into a necessary connection. Moreover, our sense of necessity is based on nothing more than the invariability of these "conjunctions" as observed in the past. If we're used to seeing one thing always following another, we tend to say that the first is *necessarily* the cause of the next. If this connection appears only occasionally, we say that one thing *may* or *can* cause the next.

The fact that events following one another are often seen as having a cause-and-effect relationship raises the issue of time, notoriously the most difficult thing to define next to consciousness itself. Augustine, writing in his *Confessions*, says, "What, then, is time? I know well enough what it is, provided nobody asks me; but if I am asked what it is and try to explain, I am baffled."[11] Nevertheless, time is sometimes defined as the measure of change, and this is reasonably satisfactory. Take this sequence of digits:

318849509483284895920932048589609**3**090…

Assuming that the sequence continues in its present fashion, we will have a 3 recurring at every eleventh space. This give us a gauge by which to measure the somewhat random occurrence of numbers in between. Here we have a sense of time in its most basic form: the measuring of more random occurrences (events in our lives, weather patterns, wars) in terms of reasonably constant ones (the circuit of the earth around the sun, the rate of decay of certain molecules).

Without an immediate gauge to measure it, time takes on a highly subjective quality. The days pass in a very different way for someone confined alone in a windowless cell than they do for someone who is free to see the sun. Similarly the amount of time that appears to pass in a dream may have nothing to do with hours and minutes on a clock. The same holds true for certain drug-induced experiences. A friend of mine told me about a time when his father was put under nitrous oxide while in the dentist's chair. He was at once transported into another life, complete with a wife and children and a house. Years seemed to pass. At one point in this other existence, he was sitting on the porch of his house, talking with a friend. Suddenly he came to in the dentist's chair. This entire alternate life had taken place within a minute or so of clock time. We could go further and say that all altered states of consciousness in one way or another distort the familiar sense of time. This is why the British psychiatrist Maurice Nicoll, a pupil of both Gurdjieff and Jung, could frame it as a rule: *"A change in the time-sense characterizes higher degrees of consciousness."*[12]

In any event, the discernment of pattern sequences underlies all our experience of the world, including scientific inquiry. A scientific formula, no matter how brilliant and intricate, is simply a means of predicting a pattern sequence of a extremely particular type.

The most influential philosopher of science in the twentieth century was undoubtedly Karl Popper. For Popper, scientific formulas and the like are not deterministic laws but hypotheses. Scientists do not posit universal causal laws: they frame hypotheses on the basis of past experience, that is, research. They then test these hypotheses against further experience, that is, more research. By this view, a scientific theory must be falsifiable. Some theories stand up well, such as the law of gravity or that of electromagnetism, having been tested and retested countless times; others are far more tenuous. But even the most widely accepted theory remains open to refutation, and refutation is always possible in the future, at least theoretically.

To understand this point, let's return to the sequence of digits shown on page 67. If you read these digits in order, not seeing which one will come next, you would start out believing that 3 always follows 5. This would be a good and sustainable hypothesis until you passed the point indicated by the slashes. At that point you would have to throw your hypothesis out and come up with another, such as one stating that 3 is always the third digit after 5. You might find this to be true for enormous strings of digits, but you would still have to face the possibility that at some point, however remote, the sequence will change. So it is with all science. In the words of parapsychologist Lawrence LeShan, "Science is truth until further notice."[13]

Moreover, there is no way of knowing for certain that any of the sequences that we call the laws of nature *will* continue in the future. Philosophers sometimes amuse themselves by speculating what would happen if all natural laws were due to cease operating after, say, January 1, 2100. Of course we cannot say that this is definitely *not* the case. If it were, the past would give no reliable indication of the future beyond that point. Bertrand Russell put the point wittily when he wrote, "The man who has fed the chicken every day throughout its life at last wrings its neck instead, showing that more refined views as to the uniformity of nature would have been useful to the chicken."[14] Or as investors read in every mutual fund prospectus, "past performance does not guarantee future results."

Hume's portrait of causation as constant conjunction no doubt seemed radical in his time, when scientists were just beginning to formulate the allegedly invariable laws of nature that were to lay the foundation for their discipline. His ideas seem less shocking today, when physicists are describing even the motions of particles in a far more indeterminate and probabilistic way than their counterparts in the past could have imagined.

At any rate, it would be hard to overstate the importance of Hume's discussion of causation to all subsequent Western philosophy. Kant wrote that his encounter with Hume "was the very thing which ... first interrupted my dogmatic slumber and gave my investigations in the field of speculative philosophy a quite new direction." From his investigations, Kant concluded that we perceive reality not directly but through the mediation of certain primary structures of experience, or as he put it, "concepts which I was now certain had not derived from experience . . . but from the pure understanding." Kant called these concepts of "the pure understanding" *categories*, of which, he said, there are twelve. They include such things as unity, plurality, totality, reality, negation, and limitation, but the most important is certainly "causality and dependence."[15] Causality is central to Kant's metaphysics. Schopenhauer went so far as to say that for Kant "the law of causality is the real, but also the only, form of the understanding, and the remaining eleven categories are merely blind windows."[16]

Kant contended that even our concept of time derives from our concept of causality and not the other way around.[17] His theory is corroborated in a curious way by physics, all of whose laws, according to mathematician Roger Penrose, "are symmetrical in time. They can be used equally well in one direction in time as in the other."[18] That is, from the point of view of elementary physical laws, it makes as much sense for a car to spontaneously assemble itself from disparate pieces as for it to fall apart into those pieces. But we don't experience time that way: we experience it as moving forward in a single direction — the "arrow of time." Consequently some other factor must be at play. Kant is saying that this other factor is the category of cause and effect as it operates in our minds. What the world is *really* like — what Kant called the *Ding an sich*, or the "thing in itself" — apart from the categories as they operate in the human mind, was, he believed, ultimately unknowable.

One could write a history of Western philosophy centered on how these concepts have fared over the centuries. The medieval

Scholastics defined truth as *adaequatio rei et intellectus*: roughly, a correlation between the thing and one's understanding of it.[19] This corresponds to the commonsense view that there is a world of objects, and that we match words up with them more or less accurately. For Kant in the eighteenth century, the object is almost completely occluded by the concept: the *Ding an sich* is at a far remove from our direct apprehension. As time passed, the *Ding*, the "thing," would disappear almost entirely — from Continental philosophy, at any rate — to be supplanted by the sign. Already in the eighteenth century, Johann Heinrich Lambert, a German philosopher and naturalist who was a correspondent of Kant's, not only coined the word *phenomenology* but also proposed to "reduce *the theory of things* to the *theory of signs*."[20] For twentieth-century postmodernists, reality is more or less equivalent to textuality: there are no objects and there is no real world, merely signifiers that have meaning only within a particular text. Invoking Heidegger, Jacques Derrida, the doyen of postmodernism, writes, "Fundamentally nothing escapes the movement of the signifier and ... in the last instance, the difference between signified and signifier is *nothing*."[21] Hence also the dictum of the French psychoanalyst Jacques Lacan that the signifier represents the subject to *another signifier*. The signified has been so completely obliterated that postmodernists regard it as naive to believe in it at all. While we can see how this philosophy arose in recent generations, with their Orwellian capacity to detach the meanings of words from objects at the whim of a despot or an advertiser, we can wonder how valid the postmodernist view is beyond the few patchy insights it offers. Certainly in the English-speaking world, with its Gradgrindian insistence on *thingness*, postmodernism has always been an exotic transplant, able to survive only in the hothouses of higher education.

The history of the influence of Hume's and Kant's ideas makes them appear to be highly at variance. Hume launched the great impulse of skepticism that would shape (and at this point cripple) Anglo-American philosophy for over two centuries. Kant's thought would lead to German idealism and to its descendant, postmodernism, with all their extravagances. At the core, however, these two philosophers said nothing radically different. Kant's formulation of the categories must have been influenced at least to some degree by these reflections about causality in Hume's *Treatise of Human Nature*: "And how much must we be disappointed, when we learn that this connexion, tie, or energy [of causation] lies merely in ourselves, and is nothing but that determination of the mind, which is acquir'd by custom, and causes us to make a transition from an object to its usual attendant, and from the impression of one to the lively idea of the other?"[22] What Hume called a "determination of the mind" Kant would refine into the theory of the categories.

These speculations involving strings of digits, categories, and so on may seem dry, so let's look at the matter from a different angle. Consider the celebrated allegory of the cave in Plato's *Republic*. In this passage, Plato's mouthpiece, Socrates, tells a story of people who have been chained in a cave from birth, with their heads fixed so that they can see only in front of them. Behind them is a fire that casts its light on the wall. People behind the prisoners are passing back and forth in front of this fire, "carrying all sorts of artefacts, . . . human statuettes, and animal models carved in stone and wood and all kinds of materials."[23] The ones who are chained, however, can see only "the shadows cast by the fire on to the cave wall directly opposite them."

At some point, one of these unfortunates is released from his chains. Finally he is able to turn his head and see the objects and the fire that has cast the shadows. He then goes up to the surface of the earth, where he can see objects in the full light of the sun. Eventually he makes his way back down to the cave to enlighten the other prisoners. Socrates goes on to say, "Suppose that the prisoners used to assign prestige and credit to one another, in the sense that they rewarded speed at recognizing the shadows as they passed, and the ability to remember which ones normally come earlier and later and at the same time as which other ones, and expertise at using this as a basis for guessing which ones would arrive next. Do you think our former prisoner would covet these honours and would envy the people who had status and power there?"[24]

Like Hume's discussion of causation, this allegory is one of the most famous texts in all of Western philosophy. Few, however, have noticed that these two passages are essentially making the same point. Hume speaks of "constant conjunction," Plato of benighted prisoners who confer honors for guessing which of the shadows is going to come next on the basis of the previous ones. In both cases, there is no causation — not, at any rate, in the familiar sense of the term. There are merely strings of events whose relation to one another is more or less arbitrary. It's merely the regularity of the sequence that we call causality; for the correct guessing of this sequence, we confer honor and status and power. Nobody, of course, is interested in forecasting the sequence of shadows on a cave wall, but if you view the matter in terms of scientific discoveries or of predicting the direction of the stock market, the situation takes on a different light.

There is, however, at least one more difficulty with Hume's view. To a great extent it portrays events in the world as discrete and separable entities, like the digits in the strings I gave earlier. And what reason do we have for supposing that events in the world are really that way? Aren't we just as right to assume that there are actually no distinct events, that the world is instead a seamless flow of one event into another? Why should we think the world is made up of dots on a line rather than of waves on a sea?

In the end, there is probably no good reason for choosing one set of metaphors over another; each one has its own particular value in highlighting certain aspects of the world as we apprehend it. There is even a curious analogy between these speculations and the scientific conundrum of why light behaves at times like a wave and at other times like a particle. Whatever the reality is behind these appearances — and any number of philosophers from Plato to Kant have contended that it's difficult if not impossible to perceive in a pure state — it can present any number of guises. Parvati can take the form of Shiva's divine consort *and* of an enticing untouchable.

This fabric of causal events — which we subdivide into discrete sections called, for example, the birth of the universe, the appearance of life on earth, the course of human history, the humdrum pattern of our own small lives, or for that matter, the sequence of terms and images that some call signifiers — is the garment of Parvati, or rather it *is* Parvati. In the language of the Samkhya, it is *prakriti*, the substance of nature, the sum total of what is perceived by consciousness in all dimensions and from all angles. As I noted earlier, the occult philosophers of the Renaissance called *prakriti* the *anima mundi*, the "soul of the world." It is how consciousness experiences the world, or rather it is what consciousness experiences *as* the world; it is how Shiva consorts with Parvati.

But haven't we painted ourselves into a corner here? I have just said that consciousness can experience the world in any number of ways, but I have also invoked Plato and Kant, both of whom stressed the mind's limitations in apprehending reality. It would seem that consciousness is multiform and illimitable, and yet very much circumscribed and even deluded.

The contradiction is only apparent. Let's grant that consciousness, *purusha*, has the freedom to experience the world from an infinite number of perspectives and dimensions. If we take this to its logical conclusion, then the range of possibilities available to it will include partial, incomplete, and even delusory states. Consciousness is not limited in any respect. It enjoys the freedom even to deceive itself, and even truth cannot fully contain it.

A far more difficult problem arises out of Hume's concept of a "determination of the mind" and Kant's theory of categories. Up to now in this book, I have characterized all that exists by carving it up into two entities: that which experiences, *purusha*, and that which is experienced, *prakriti*. Now we see that the matter is not quite so simple. There is not only the experiencer and the experience but also the *mode* of experience — the way in which mind apprehends the world. For Hume the key factor here is the law of association; for Kant it is the categories. As Kant understood, you will find it very hard to imagine a world apart from these categories. A world without unity or plurality? A world without limitation or negation or causality? Even the wildest science-fiction writer has never attempted to portray an alternate reality so incommensurably unlike our own. Similarly it's almost impossible to conceive of an intelligence of any sort that does not somehow make use of associations, as Hume no doubt would have acknowledged.

As soon as we begin to look into these modes of awareness, however, we realize that they are double-edged. They both enable consciousness to perceive the world and limit that very perception. Kant did not believe it possible ever to experience what he called the *noumenon*, the *Ding an sich* or "thing in itself," that exists apart from the categories. Plato believed in the ideas or forms, the archetypes of all things that exist in the world of pure intelligence far above the realm of sensation. This world of pure intelligence is, in the allegory of the cave, the surface of the earth to which the freed prisoner is led with some reluctance. Plato certainly considered it possible to experience the forms cognitively, through logic and dialectics and perhaps through other means, but he didn't say it was easy to accomplish. Until we can do this, he contended, we remain chained in the cave, bewitched by shadows.

This throws us back on another theme we've already touched on: the idea of *maya*, or illusion, or as the Buddhists call it, *samsara*. For the Advaita Vedantins, *maya* consists of experiencing this world in discrete bits, isolated from the atman, or Self, of cognition, rather than as the harmonious whole that it is (at least theoretically), in which perceiver and perceived are one.

How does this illusion arise? As we've already seen, if consciousness is illimitable, it paradoxically retains the capacity even to be deluded and deceived by *maya*. Although the precise mechanism of how this happens is extremely subtle and hard to grasp, it has been described by a number of sacred traditions, particularly those of India. And it casts the issue of causation in a new and entirely different light.

In the beginning, all is consciousness. At the same time, all is unconsciousness. Why? If we define consciousness as the capacity to define self and other, at this primordial stage there *is* no self or other. Hence mystics have frequently used opaque and paradoxical language to describe this condition. Here is one example, from the creation hymn of the Rig Veda:

> There was neither non-existence nor existence then; there was
> neither the realm of space nor the sky which is beyond. What

stirred? Where? In whose protection? Was there water, bot-
tomlessly deep?

There was no distinguishing sign of night nor of day. That
one breathed, windless, by its own impulse. Other than that
there was nothing beyond.[25]

From a superficial point of view, this is merely mystical mumbo
jumbo, but from the point of view of what we've just been examining, it's relatively clear. Without self and other, there is "neither
non-existence nor existence"; neither is there death and immortality, or day and night. The book of Genesis, too, speaks of the
time before creation when "the earth was without form and void;
and darkness was on the face of the deep" (Genesis 1:2). It would
be easy to add examples from countless other sacred texts.

At some point — and this is not a historical event that occurred
once in the unfathomable past but something that takes place
moment by moment, with each sliver of experience — a distinction arises. Genesis puts it in terms of dividing the "waters above"
from the "waters below" and of separating night and day (a curious parallel to the Rig Veda's "no distinguishing sign of night nor
of day"; indeed, there are a number of parallels between this Vedic
hymn and the opening of Genesis). Out of the primordial abyss a
slight, subtle, almost embryonic distinction begins to arise. There
is an experience; with it comes almost instantaneously an experiencer: consequently we have self and other, and consciousness. As
the *Samkhyakarika* puts it, "From *prakriti* (emerges) the great one
(*mahat* or *buddhi*); from that (comes) *ahamkara*."[26] *Buddhi* means
cognition or understanding; *ahamkara* literally means "I am–ness"
— that is, a sense of "I" or self. Out of the experience of *prakriti*
by *purusha* comes the duality of self and other: "the only cause is
for the sake of the *purusa*."[27]

To disentangle some sense from this thicket of words, we can start by saying that *purusha* is extremely passive. It potentiates *prakriti* by cognizing the world, but it does nothing else. So how can it affect the world? Only by its cognition. All action, all movement, all of what calls itself *will* is the ceaseless dynamic of *prakriti*, the motivating energy of which the Hindu philosophers call *shakti*. *Purusha* bestows this power by its mere act of cognition, and it does nothing else. This act instantaneously produces a pure and immediate distinction of self and other, which the Samkhya calls *buddhi*.

Buddhi is usually translated as "intellect" or "intuition," but these are bad choices. In fact there is no good English equivalent. *Buddhi* is much subtler and more profound than either intellect or intuition in their usual senses. Perhaps the best way to give some notion of *buddhi* is through a Kabbalistic concept that I believe is very closely related: Binah, the third *sefirah* (or principle) of the Kabbalistic Tree of Life. Usually this is translated as "understanding," but again this is not quite right. The Kabbalists say that Binah is derived from the Hebrew preposition *ben*, which simply means "between." Consequently Binah is the primordial distinction, the primordial "between." This primordial distinction is between self and other. With this cognitive step, a certain polarity, a sense of "here" and "there," begins to gel, and, in the words of James Joyce, "a world that was not comes to pass."

The most common experience of *buddhi* occasionally occurs immediately after waking in the morning. You sometimes find that you are alert and feeling refreshed. There is a sense that everything is all right. There are no problems, no difficulties. All is clear and new. There is consciousness, there is a sense of self and other, of here and there, but it is unimpeded; it presents no problems. But very soon — and I am talking about seconds rather than minutes

— you realize something is missing, and you begin groping for it, as if you knew you could not get up without it. You remember where you are in the world; your problems, hopes, appetites, duties all come flooding in on you. Your sense of self, your "I-formation," has been restored. In the language of the Samkhya, you have moved from *buddhi* into *ahamkara* or "I am–ness." For the most part, it is not a pleasant experience. To use the language of esoteric Christianity, it is a fall into a world that will present you with plenty of both good and evil.

Buddhi, then, gives rise to *ahamkara*, the fundamental sense of "I." At this point your experience congeals into what is usually called the ego; the freshness of consciousness at the moment of wakening freezes into a personality with wishes and desires and problems. As one scholar says, it is "the mind as active I becoming the standing me."[28] Now *purusha* is fixed by its identification with *prakriti*. It clutches onto a small segment of *prakriti*'s measureless stream and calls it its own — or rather, calls it *me*. Like Narcissus, it falls in love with its own reflection in the ceaselessly churning world of experience and is drowned. Or, like Ialdabaoth, the second-rate deity whom the Gnostics say molded our defective universe, it says, "I am and there is no other beside me." Experience becomes *my* experience.

Buddhi produces *ahamkara*: the distinction between self and other generates an "I." This gives rise to events in the psychic realm: thoughts, images, mental constructs. The Samkhya calls this *manas*, which is mind as we usually understand it. The English word *mind* is derived from the Latin *mens*. Even on the printed page, *manas* and *mens* look remarkably similar, and in fact they come from the same Indo-European root. *Manas* is the sum total of thoughts, emotions, cognitions, images, and dreams, conscious and unconscious, that pass across the screen of the psyche.

Manas is your customary state of mind, and it arises whenever *ahamkara* is present. In terms of moment-to-moment experience, *manas* is the stream of thoughts that the ego produces as a strategy for self-perpetuation. The thoughts that go through your mind are almost entirely means used by *ahamkara*, the ego, to hold itself together. Some of these are basic survival strategies: Where will I get my next meal? How can I make more money? Others are concerned with the ego's status in the world: What do they think of me? How can I look good in these circumstances? Such is *manas* in waking life. But even in dreaming, if we believe Freud and his school, a great deal of the activity of the dreaming mind is in service to the ego's self-concept.

As soon as *ahamkara* and *manas* arise, they become problematic and even painful. The *Samkhyakarika* alludes to this fact in its opening verse: "Because of the torment of the threefold suffering, (there arises) the desire to know the means of removing it."[29] Buddhists will recognize a powerful echo here of the Four Noble Truths: the existence of suffering, the cause of suffering, the fact that suffering can be ended, and the means of ending it. Moreover, the "threefold suffering" looks very much like the Three Poisons of Buddhism: desire, anger, and obliviousness. The resemblances are so strong that the Samkhya is accounted as one of the chief influences on the Buddha's teaching.

Why is suffering threefold? Why are there three poisons and not two or four? The answer is simple: once you have constellated the world into this dichotomy of self and other, you (the "self") have only three ways of responding to the other: you can move toward it; you can move away from it; or you can do neither. These are the only possibilities available in the world as we know it. In the language of Buddhism, the first is desire, the second aversion, and the third obliviousness.

The Samkhya does not portray this ternary in exactly the same way, but it comes close. It speaks of the three *gunas*: *sattva*, equilibrium; *rajas*, excitement; and *tamas*, inertia. The Sanskrit word *guna* is usually translated as "quality," although it also means "rope": the *gunas* are the ropes that bind consciousness to its own experience.[30] According to the Samkhya, these *gunas* generate the entirety of manifest existence, just as the Buddhists say that all of *samsara* results from the operation of the Three Poisons, and Christians believe that the universe is created by the Trinity.

This intricate chain of manifestation can seem remote to us. As a matter of fact, it is the opposite; as the prophet Muhammad said of Allah, it is closer than your jugular vein. You do not see this process because it happens instantaneously, on a moment-by-moment basis, and you take it utterly for granted. In the most mercilessly literal sense, you don't know what you would be without it. This is partly why the sages have insisted so strongly on meditation as a necessity for awakening. By stilling and calming the mind, meditation slows down this process of I-formation so that some of its steps can be seen and thereby loosened, and so that *purusha*, pure consciousness, can begin to be freed. (The sages of the Samkhya did not agree that meditation was necessary, by the way; they held that mere cognitive insight into the situation was enough to ensure liberation.)

The sages of the Samkhya would agree with Hume that the phenomenal world is merely a string of occurrences that, strictly speaking, have no causal connection with one another.[31] What *is* causative are the *gunas*, which in turn arise ultimately out of the dynamic between *purusha* and *prakriti*, between Shiva and his capricious bride. But the *gunas* cannot be apprehended in their pure form. You can never see pure *sattva* or *rajas* or *tamas*: they are visible only in their manifestations and combinations, just as in

Christianity the Trinity cannot be seen except in the mirror of creation.

This whole discussion reveals causation to us in two guises. One, the conventional view, is totally flat and linear: it amounts to nothing more than recognizing sequences of events. Metaphorically, it is the discernment of repeating digits in a string of numbers, or guessing which out of a series of shadows will appear next on the cave wall. The human mind has become extremely clever in perceiving causation in this sense. It can predict when apples on a tree will ripen or where a particle will go if it is struck with a certain amount of force. But as Hume saw, this kind of causation is nothing more than an elaborate sense of constant conjunction. If we understand these conjunctions thoroughly enough, we will understand causation of the familiar sort. At the same time, nothing in this titanic string of events gives us any clue to why or how the string came about to begin with. Aristotle's First Cause, an unmoved mover who in some incomprehensible way began the sequence without having a beginning himself, is no more plausible an explanation than the Samkhya's view that this string is beginningless and endless.

Such is the conventional type of causation. It does not and cannot offer any real notion of God, because God here could be nothing more than another cipher in the string of events. As we've seen, God has sometimes been inserted into this string as a placeholder, an unseen agent intervening between events that cannot otherwise be explained. But this cannot be God in the real meaning of the word, if only because a simpler and more immediate agency can usually be found. After electricity was discovered, we no longer needed Zeus to stand in as the creator of thunder. God will not be found in this causal chain.

If, however, we see causation in a deeper sense as the ceaseless interplay of *purusha* and *prakriti*, the matter takes on another guise. *Buddhi*, *ahamkara*, and the *gunas* arise out of this interplay, and they are the true causes of manifestation. While the Samkhya enumeration is by no means identical to Kant's theory of the categories, they share one crucial element: both of them focus on how the world — our world, the world we see and take for granted as real — is generated by the limits and structures of consciousness. For Kant, these include such things as identity, unity, and causation; in the Samkhya, they are the capacities for thought and sense and action generated by a consciousness that has fallen into a frozen and isolated sense of itself.

Where, then, is God? As we saw in the previous chapter, God can be experienced both as self (*purusha*) and as other (*prakriti*). Ultimately, however, the true God is beyond and above both self and other; God is the unfathomable reality that gives rise to this divine game. The Samkhya does not speak directly of this unfathomable reality; consequently it is sometimes (and not entirely accurately) characterized as atheistic. Other traditions, however, do make mention of this reality. God is the *Urgrund*, the "primordial ground," of the medieval German mystic Meister Eckhart; the Ain Soph, or "infinity," of the Kabbalists; the Nirguna Brahman ("Brahman without qualities") of the Hindus. That this reality has been encountered and described so many times by so many great visionaries is one, but only one, testimony to its truth.

PATTERNS IN HER GARMENT
The Chain of Associations

The reflections in the previous chapter have raised a complication. Up to that point the scheme that I've been outlining had a remarkable simplicity: all that there is consists of consciousness and experience. Now we have found that something else is involved: the modes or ways in which consciousness engages with its experience. We may think of these modes in terms of Kant's categories, of the Samkhya enumeration, or of any number of other systems. But the upshot is the same: mind as we know it is structured to experience the world in certain ways. This fact imposes certain limitations upon it.

Mystical literature tends to decry these limitations, insisting that mind is born free but is everywhere in chains. The nature of *maya*, according to the Advaita Vedanta, centers on this truth. *Maya* makes us see the world as a heap of separate and isolated objects, when in fact they are all one. Similarly the Samkhya says that *ahamkara*, I-formation, is the cause of the apparent bondage of *purusha* to its own experience.

Consider your moment-to-moment experience. Right now you are reading a book. To the extent that you're paying attention to what you're doing, you are unaware of any number of other things that are going on around you. If you are in a room, your awareness of the furniture, the light, and the atmosphere is dimmed. If you are at the seashore, you are comparatively blind to the ocean, the wind, and the sand. But if you turn your attention to these things, you will lose your awareness of the book you're reading. It would seem that you can't have it both ways.

The capacity of consciousness to limit itself must be accompanied by the corresponding capacity to expand, since a consciousness that could only limit itself without expanding would be forced, in the short or long term, to dwindle away to nothing. So these are two properties of consciousness: *expansion* and *limitation*. You can easily see this too in your moment-to-moment experience. Assuming you are completely focused on this book, again raise your eyes and take in your surroundings. Previously you were more or less unaware of them as you were reading; now your consciousness expands to include the whole of your environs. You can also easily let this awareness drop and focus on the book again. This process of limiting and expanding consciousness is something we do every instant, almost always without being aware of it.

Various forms of meditation are designed to hone the mind's capacity for expansion and contraction. To be able to focus — that is, limit — the mind is the essence of concentration. Concentration is fixing your mind on a particular point to the exclusion of all others. Although it is a constraint, it's also an extremely valuable skill to have, since the mind is usually restless and distracted; to some extent we are all prone to attention deficit disorder. Practices aimed at overcoming this distractedness include focusing the attention on a mantra, a prayer, a visual image, the breath, or the sensations of the body to the exclusion of all else. The mind is given an extremely limited area in which it's free to move. If you do these practices well, you will be *unaware* of many more things than you are aware of. This is extremely difficult to do: for all but the most advanced practitioners, any number of irrelevant thoughts and feelings will constantly intrude. Two Tibetan lamas write:

> Of course, it naturally happens when you meditate that thoughts suddenly arise and lead you in different directions. When you see that happening, rather than following the thoughts, immediately bring the mind back through mindfulness. The reason you need to meditate is because concepts have covered up the natural state [of the mind]. If thoughts did not cause confusion, you would not need to meditate. However, you should not be upset or sad when thoughts arise. It is quite normal for thoughts to arise during meditation. The main point is not to follow the thoughts.[1]

The mind that is focused in this way becomes sharp and intense like a laser. In Tibetan Buddhism, one of the most common metaphors for this power of mind is the diamond: something perfectly clear and pure and hard, something capable of cutting through all other things without itself suffering damage.

By contrast, meditative practices that are intended to expand the range of consciousness are not as numerous, perhaps because they're still more difficult and usually presuppose some expertise in concentration. Methods of expanding consciousness include Zen sitting and the *rigpa* practice of the Dzogchen tradition of Tibet, in which one simply rests in pure awareness. The mind focuses on nothing and excludes nothing; thoughts and sensations may come and go like reflections on a crystal mirror. The spirit of this practice is expressed in the brief Dzogchen text known as the *Six Vajra Verses*:

The nature of phenomena is nondual,
but each one, in its own state, is beyond
the limits of the mind.
There is no concept that can define
the condition of "what is"
but vision nevertheless manifests:
all is good.
Everything has already been accomplished,
and so, having overcome the sickness of effort,
one finds oneself in the self-perfected state:
this is contemplation.[2]

Another property of consciousness is implied by the definition I gave at the beginning of this book. If consciousness is the ability to relate self and other, this must entail the capacity to *distinguish*, to say "this" and "not this." This capacity is not limited to the primordial distinction between self and other; it can also distinguish many "others," which it then sees as separate things and events. Collectively these are what we call the world.

The property complementary to this ability to distinguish is the capacity to see similarities, to *liken*. If you are able to look up at a tree and recognize it as a tree, this is largely because you have seen trees before and know what they are. Recognition, along with memory, is largely a function of the capacity to see similarities. If you'd never seen a tree before, you would be able (probably) to perceive it as distinct from its background, but you would not know it as a tree.

This principle is illustrated in stories of primitive tribes confronted with the artifacts of civilization. Supposedly only the wise men of the Arawak tribe in the West Indies were able to see the ships of Columbus as they appeared on the horizon in 1492; at first, tribesmen of ordinary intelligence, having never seen such things as ships before, could not see those of Columbus. I'm reminded of another story about some Bedouins who had never seen representative drawing. When a European traveler drew a sketch of one of them, the Bedouin could make nothing of it at all. The European pressed him a little, and finally, seeing the vaguely rounded shape of his own head on the paper, the Bedouin guessed that it might be a camel. Clark Wissler, an early-twentieth-century anthropologist of American Indians, describes a similar experience:

> The old Indian of my day experienced difficulty in recognizing any kind of a picture. This seems strange to us, brought up amidst pictures, but I recall how when one of these old timers was shown his photograph he scowled at it, turned it first one way and the other, finally in desperation biting it. I came to the rescue by putting the card in the correct position, then pointing out the eyes, nose, mouth, etc. After a time he seemed to grasp it, but was obviously disappointed by so poor a representation.[3]

As weird as these stories may sound, we can wonder how our own preconceptions limit our perception. Take the countless sightings of UFOs, monsters, spirits, and beings from other realms. Is it possible that our explanations of these things are so contrived and implausible because we can't relate them to our own memories of objects in the world we know? Some liken these apparitions to the nearest objects in their experience — hence "flying saucers" — while others of perhaps lower intelligence simply fall back and deny that these things exist at all.

In any case, these modes — the ability to expand and contract, to distinguish and liken — are among the most basic features that consciousness possesses. If Schopenhauer were alive, we might be able to convince even him that these features are not merely blind windows. As I've already pointed out, much of what I say in this book echoes Schopenhauer's thought, and if he had titled his magnum opus *The World as Consciousness and Representation* instead of *The World as Will and Representation*, he and I might have been close to saying the same thing. But the fact that he called his work what he did brings up another, more problematic aspect of these issues. While Schopenhauer did admit the presence of a universal subject — what the Samkhya calls *purusha* — he was far more interested in *will*, that is, how this subject acts or appears to act in the world. The views I've sketched out here, by contrast, may make consciousness appear passive: they explain how it *apprehends* the world, but they don't go far toward explaining how it *acts* in the world.

It's not my purpose to give a detailed critique of Schopenhauer; I'm merely mentioning him to suggest how what I am arguing compares to his thought. But this question of how consciousness acts in the world leads to its final and most problematic feature as I understand it. This is the capacity to *identify* with its experience. As Gerald J. Larson says in discussing the Samkhya, "If consciousness is only a contentless passive presence, it can only appear as what it is not, passively taking on all content (whether subjective or objective) as a transparent witness."[4] This content would of course include activity, so *purusha*, under the delusion of *ahamkara*, comes to believe that it possesses will. But all activity and will belong to *prakriti*. Consciousness does not act. It only seems to act.

Nevertheless, there are degrees of identification. The more *purusha* is identified with its experience, the more deluded and impotent it is. The less it is identified, the more enlightened and empowered it becomes. The degree of identification can vary, and these degrees sift experience into different strata.

This brings our discussion to the different levels of existence — one of the central themes of nearly all esoteric literature. Moreover, the descriptions correspond in a general way even if they differ on details. The Samkhya's enumerations (which extend far beyond the basic twenty-five that I described in the previous chapter) are a bit dry and analytical and may not be as illuminating as others. The Kabbalah, for example, speaks of four worlds: Atziluth, the divine world; Briah, the world of creation; Yetzirah, the world of formation; Assiyah, the world of physical action. But merely to set out these terms, and even to explain them, may seem artificial to the reader who is not already disposed to believe in them. They're easily written off as mystical mumbo jumbo. For this reason, it's useful to approach the matter from another angle — by going back to the features of reality as conventionally understood, which I outlined in chapter 2. As I said there, to be taken as real, an experience must be stable, stereoscopic, publicly accessible, encountered in waking life, and more or less in accord with our preconceptions.

However tenuous or delusory it may ultimately prove, this is the world of "reality" that we take for granted. If we analyze it fully, it ends up being more or less identical with the physical world. In fact, as I've already stressed, reality and "thingness" are, to our everyday mentality, practically identical. As soon as we've said this, however, we're forced to admit that there is a whole realm of experience that is characterized as unreal because it refuses to answer to one or more of the familiar criteria for reality.

There is a paradox here. What is real in the ultimate sense, according to the esoteric teachings, is, from the naturalistic point of view, unreal, and vice versa. "Lead us from the unreal to the real," says a prayer in the Upanishads.[5] "What we see when our eyes are open is death; what we see when we dream is waking life," says the famously obscure Greek philosopher Heraclitus.[6]

But to avoid confusion, let's stay with the conventional view, at least for now. What to do with the "unreal" dimension of subjective life is far from clear, at least to the contemporary Western mind. On the one hand, it is not accepted as "true" in the sense that physical phenomena are. On the other hand, we can't dismiss it entirely. Dreams, hunches, intuitions, hallucinations, visions, encounters with gods and devils — these are the stuff of human experience every bit as much as are sticks and stones and dollar bills. Reductionistic explanations have never accounted for them; if they've tried to, the explanation inevitably sounds forced and factitious. You had a dream because your brain cells were firing in a certain way during REM sleep — very well, what does that amount to? When you were awake, you saw a tree outside because your brain cells were firing in another, quite different way; why should the same explanation invalidate the experience in one case and not in the other? Recent years have seen various attempts to similarly explain away religious experience. There are evidently certain areas of the brain that you can prod with an electrode so that the subject will see God. Again, very well; but there are other centers you can poke that will make the subject see stars or flashes of light, and no one concludes from this that visual phenomena as a whole are unreal. Quite the opposite: the capacity in the brain to have such experiences would, prima facie, count as stronger evidence *for* the existence of the phenomena associated with those experiences than against it. We have light receptors in the brain because there is such a thing as light. Perhaps we have "God" receptors in the brain because there is such a thing as God.

All this is to say that the "unreal" cannot be explained away so easily. These allegedly unreal experiences are the product of certain brain states; but then, so are the explanations that endeavor to refute them. It might be wiser not to dismiss these "unreal" experiences but to try to understand them — and this of course requires applying a set of laws and concepts different from the one we would apply to physical phenomena.

The esoteric philosophies of the world have devoted an enormous amount of literature to this realm of the "unreal." They have also given names to it. The name of the lowest level (apart from the purely physical) has already appeared in this chapter: Yetzirah, the ʼ ᵗʰᵉ world of forms, which can include any-

ᵉriences with ghosts

ᵑ call it the astral

h these images

en on the most

with the stars and

planets. ᴅᵤᵗ ᵗ of *rupa*, or "form," as opposed to the physiᵤᵤ ᵢd of *kama*, "desire." The most universal name for it in our civilization is the *psyche*. Your psyche consists of the totality of thoughts, images, and feelings that have ever registered, consciously or unconsciously, on the screen of your mind.

Nearly all esoteric schools postulate levels of reality beyond even this comparatively familiar realm. The Kabbalists, as we've seen, have Briah and Atziluth; for the Buddhists, these constitute the *arupa*, or "formless" realm, which is so subtle that, as its name suggests, its contents do not have form, although they still possess a tenuous sense of self and other that places them in the sphere of manifestation. But these dimensions are so far out of the range of ordinary experience that we should set them aside for now.

We can see that these many levels of being are based on precise calibrations of the primordial capacities of consciousness that I have sketched out. We are capable of expanding and contracting our field of attention, but only to a degree; we are capable of seeing both differences and similarities, but only within highly circumscribed limits, and so on. If these settings, so to speak, are changed even a little, the state of consciousness changes dramatically.

Take the most familiar of the altered states of consciousness: the dream state. This bears a certain resemblance to waking awareness. There is a sense of self and other, a sense of similarity and dissimilarity, and so on, but these are all set just differently enough that the dream state is wildly at odds with waking life. It's the commonest thing in the world to hear someone say, "I had a strange dream last night"; but no one ever says, "I had a perfectly normal dream last night." In the words of one authority quoted by Freud, "Out of every ten dreams, the content of at least nine is absurd."[7] Probably even this is a conservative estimate. Some of this absurdity is unquestionably due to differences in the calibrations of consciousness.

Perhaps the most important of these differences is in the capacities to distinguish and liken. These are not the same in dreams as in waking life. In the latter, the law of the excluded middle prevails. Everything either is or is not. Either the stove is on or it isn't. Either that is a tree or it isn't. Either something is green or it is not (even something that's just a little bit green is still green). Most critically, you are not me, nor are you the same as another, third person. In the dream state, this is not the case. Most people can find examples from their own experience, but here is one from literature. At the opening of Tolstoy's *Anna Karenina*, Prince Stepan Oblonsky wakes up on a sofa in the study, where he has had to sleep after a fight with his wife.

> "Let's see, let's see, how was it?" he said to himself as he tried
> to recall his dream. "How was it, now? Ah, yes! Alabin had us
> to dinner in Darmstadt; no, not Darmstadt...something American...no, this Darmstadt was in America! That's it, Alabin

gave a dinner on glass tables and — I'll be dashed if the tables didn't sing! *Il mio tesoro*, no, not *Il mio tesoro* ... something even better ... and pretty little wine-glasses ... and the wine-glasses were ladies ..." he recalled.

Oblonsky's eyes twinkled merrily and he smiled as he gave himself up to his dream. "Very jolly. Very. Lots of other nice things too, but you can't put it all into words or even thoughts, can't express it when you wake up."[8]

This is the dream state, where Darmstadt can be in America and wineglasses can also be ladies. If we calibrate the mind so that "different" and "same" are construed to be even the tiniest bit at variance with what we consider normal, very strange things start to happen.

The dream world — the most familiar world in which this slightly different notion of "different" and "same" applies — can be equated with the astral plane, Yetzirah, or the Buddhist realm of *rupa*, form. The dream world is merely a subsection of this plane. As I pointed out in the previous chapter, the Samkhya says that, when the force known as *sattva* predominates, it produces events of this kind in the realm of *manas*. One of the most common and universal symbols for this realm is water, because, unlike the physical realm, which has a comparatively high amount of stability and predictability, this subjective realm is highly fluid and unstable. An image both is and is not something else, or it can easily change into something else, as everyone, like Prince Oblonsky, has experienced in dreams. This fact helps explain the elusive and many-faceted nature of symbols, which exist in this realm.

Much of the magical and occult traditions — which make great use of symbols — has to do with familiarizing oneself with the Yetziratic plane. If this is a difficult enterprise, it is largely because of the mind's own fluidity and resistance to holding on to any given form. If I were to ask you to imagine a red rose, you would have little trouble doing so, but if I were to ask you to keep that image steadily on the screen of your mind for even five minutes, chances are you would find it hard or impossible. You would be irresistibly tempted to drift off into thinking of something else that the rose reminded you of — the rose you sent to a girlfriend once, which in turn would lead to memories of that girlfriend, which would lead to the time of your life when you were involved with her, which would lead to thoughts of where you were living then, and so on. Only a few seconds would need to pass before you would utterly forget your initial task and your mind would wander far afield. Everyone who has tried to meditate can readily verify these facts.

This characteristic of *manas* leads us to formulate the principal rule by which it operates, which is as fundamental to this realm as the elementary laws of physics are to the world of materiality. This world of forms is organized by *associations*, though of an apparently more fluid and chaotic sort than govern the realm of physical causality. In the world of images, one thing is connected to another — one thing indeed may *be* another, as in Oblonsky's dream — by this process of associations, some of which are highly personal and individual, some of which are collective or possibly universal.

The chief authorities I could invoke here are Freud and Jung, whose psychologies, profound as they are, are in sum little more than elaborate investigations of the process of association. The pages of Freud's masterwork *The Interpretation of Dreams* are filled with intricate descriptions of the chain of association in the dreams of Freud and his patients. The material analyzed by Jung is more universal, because he was investigating images that have significance for humanity as a whole — hence his term the "collective unconscious" — but the same principle still holds.

For another seminal twentieth-century figure, G. I. Gurdjieff, associations are manacles that shackle the mind of man to the waking sleep of everyday life. To understand what Gurdjieff means, again we need do nothing more than examine our own moment-to-moment experience. You are driving on the highway and you pass a billboard advertising a certain brand of vodka. Entirely without intending to, your mind drifts off to your thoughts about this brand. You may think it's overpriced, in which case your mind may lead you into a long, inner tirade about the ubiquitous commercialism and greed of our sorry age. Or you may remember that you haven't had a martini in weeks and decide that a martini might taste very good now, so you may start thinking about the next time you will go to a bar or make a cocktail for yourself at home. Or you may remember how you binged on vodka when you were in college, got horribly sick, and have never wanted to touch the stuff again. This process can easily become so absorbing that your driving becomes automatic and you're barely thinking about what you are doing. Usually this works well enough (much of our routine activity being automatic anyway), but if you're unusually absorbed in this chain of thoughts, you could miss your exit or get into an accident. Such is the sleep of man. On the other hand, if you make a point of concentrating on what you're doing, paying attention to every movement your hands and feet make with the wheel and pedals, you may become extremely bored and drift off to sleep. The momentum of associations is the chief engine firing the engine of the psyche, and when it slows down, sleep in the literal sense may step in. But more likely something else on the road will catch your attention, and the chain of associations will recommence. We use the term *chain of associations* as a kind of metaphor for endless linking of one thought to another, but thoughts are a chain in another sense too: they constitute the chief form of bondage for the mind.

Many spiritual traditions, including Buddhism and Gurdjieff's own teaching, recommend mindfulness or self-remembering as a way to counteract the mind's propensity to daydream. But even someone who has worked for a long time to strengthen her attention may well find that at best she will be able to interrupt this chain of associations and "be here now" only momentarily before the endless surge of images and thoughts commences again.

Of course the point of such practices is not to stop the flow of thoughts and images, which is probably no more feasible than stopping the tides of the sea. Instead it's frequently a matter of subtly detaching your consciousness, *purusha*, from the eternal flow of *prakriti*'s images and illusions. Normally, of course, we think they are *our* images, but this is part of the illusion. With a certain amount of practice, you can watch them impartially, as a film that passes before the mind's eye, and realize that they are no more *you* than the stream of images that flowed before your eyes last night when you went to the movies. The Self is *not* its experience; it can stand back and watch that experience, so it must be something different. This is one of the fundamental lessons of most esoteric teachings, and many of their texts are hard to understand unless you grasp this point.

In light of the previous chapter, this account of associations may have a familiar ring. After all, what we saw there as the mainstay of causation — "constant conjunction" — is little more than a specialized version of the law of associations. This fact is remarkably revealing. Even our understanding of cause and effect — without which all scientific theories, however rigorous, collapse into dust — is merely a result of the mind's capacity to associate. Moreover, the mind cannot *help* associating. As we have already seen, it's practically impossible to stop the flow of thoughts for more than a few seconds at a time. Associations, whether they take the form of the haphazard flow of images across the screen of the mind, or of the ostensibly rigid laws of cause and effect, are the primary mode by which our minds structure reality.

We could take this argument in the direction of scientific materialism. We could say that the mind forms associations because of the way neurons are linked to one another or because this proved to be a successful strategy for biological survival. This is no doubt true to a great extent. But it's more interesting to reflect that this process of association forms one of the chief filters by which consciousness is constricted in life as we know it. These modes of apprehension — such as the capacities to liken and to distinguish — give the mind a means of understanding the world, but they also block it from understanding the world more deeply.

Astrophysicists have been telling us in recent years that as much as 97 percent of the universe is composed of dark matter and dark energy, whose gravitational influences on galaxies can be observed, but which cannot themselves be observed by any known means.[9] That is, only 3 percent of the mass of the universe can be perceived by human senses or by extensions of them (such as telescopes and so on). Whatever the nature of this dark matter may be, these facts show that what our minds and our senses apprehend is only a tiny fraction of what actually exists. Even here we have some oblique notion of dark matter, and possibly science will someday explain it. But what else exists that is so far beyond the limits of the mind that we can have no inkling of it whatsoever?

Science is, of course, agnostic about such things. But it's sobering to consider that the very structures of the mind that have enabled it to understand physical reality as it does may in the end make a more comprehensive understanding of it impossible. Causation can explain the world only to a highly limited degree. If it were the only mode by which the mind could perceive, causation would be an impassable barrier. Nonetheless, the entire collective experience of the human race suggests that the realm of physical cause and effect is only one of innumerable levels of reality — and the capacity to think in terms of cause and effect is only one of innumerable ways of apprehending reality. The mind can go further, but it does so at the risk of losing its explanations. These take the form of words and sentences or mathematical formulae. And these are of necessity cast in terms of the associative reasoning that created them. If we are to free our minds to explore the universe in a more comprehensive way, these are the chains that we must cast off.

The principal means of freeing the mind is meditation. Of course, meditation is a broad category encompassing a number of practices whose purposes often differ greatly from one another. We already saw as much in this chapter when we looked at practices that either focus or expand the mind. Certain other types — and there are many — are intended to detach the mind from its own experience. Such practices may achieve similar results even when they work from diametrically opposed theories. Gurdjieff's tradition has a type of meditation known simply as "sitting," which focuses the attention on the sensations of the body. On the surface, this practice may look as if it were designed to do anything but promote detachment, and yet long experience of it can lead to awareness of what Gurdjieff called "real I," which can witness the sensations of the body without being identified with them. The *vipassana* (insight) meditation of Theravada Buddhism is very similar — so similar that Gurdjieff's followers are occasionally described as practicing *vipassana*. But Gurdjieff's teaching emphasizes *integration* of the consciousness with the body rather than detachment, which is generally seen as one of the objectives of *vipassana*. For me personally, it was the practice of Gurdjieffian sitting over the course of several years that led me to insights that, as this book testifies, are very similar to those of the Samkhya.[10] (The Samkhya does not have a meditative practice as such; rational inquiry into the "enumeration" is supposed to confer liberation, at least according to the textbooks.)

To grasp some of the dynamics of meditation, we might return to a point made earlier in this chapter: the degrees of identification constitute our experience of reality. If this is so, and if meditation is designed to weaken this identification, the meditator's consciousness will pass through many stages of experience — "many mansions," in the words of Christ — as he continues the practice. This is exactly what happens. Meditation, in fact, is so closely connected with altered states of consciousness that many believe this is the sole purpose of the practice. But it is not. Because meditation's purpose is often the detachment of *purusha* (however that's understood), teachers often instruct their students to ignore any phenomena that may arise, no matter how alluring or apparently holy. One story tells of a Buddhist master whose student ran into his room crying, "I was meditating just now, and I had a vision of the Buddha!" "Just keep meditating and it will go away" was the reply.

If the purpose of the practice were to see the Buddha, the master would never say such a thing. But because its purpose is to take consciousness past the many stages of identification, anything seductive or "interesting" — even a vision of the supreme master himself — is a distraction and a snare.

All the same, the collective experience of mystics over the centuries has produced a huge amount of material describing these planes. Shamanism has its upper and lower realms; Christianity has its hells and purgatories and heavens; the Buddhists have their six *lokas*, or realms of existence: those of the gods, *asuras* or "titans," humans, animals, beings in hell, and *pretas* or "hungry ghosts." Some remarkable individuals have generated their own cosmologies. The eighteenth-century Swedish visionary Emanuel Swedenborg produced lengthy and verbose accounts of his visits to heaven, hell, and the realm of spirits in between. More recently, the indefatigable out-of-body traveler Robert Monroe not only chronicled his experiences in the astral realms in several books but also established the Monroe Institute in Faber, Virginia, to teach others how to do the same.

Among the strangest and most haunting visions in recent times are those of Daniel Andreev (1906–59). The son of a noted Russian playwright, Andreev was accused of plotting against the Stalinist state in 1947 and sentenced to the gulag. During his ten years in prison, Andreev experienced a number of visions in which he attained what he called "transphysical knowledge." His widow, Alla Andreeva, has summarized his worldview: "For Andreev, the universe is many layered. The plane inhabited by humanity, *Enrof*, in Andreev's terms, is the middle plane. Above stretch the shining Worlds of Enlightenment, while the dark Worlds of Retribution oppose them from below. All religious cosmologies contain a structure of the universe of this kind: for instance, the Vale of Life, Hell, and Paradise in Christianity; Midgard, Niffleheim, and Asgard of Scandinavian mythology; and the Seven Heavens of Islam. Andreev's Worlds of Enlightenment and Retribution develop the same structure."[11]

It would be pointless to try to summarize the whole of Andreev's extravagant, baroque, and sublime vision; it's set out in his *Rose of the World*, first published in Russia in 1989, thirty years after his death. Nonetheless, a few details are relevant here. This is his description of one of his purgatories, or "Worlds of Retribution": "In the meantime the mouth of the stream can be seen up ahead. The stream itself, and the entire tunnel-shaped world, breaks off just as a subway tunnel breaks off where a trestle begins. But the water does not fall anywhere: the water and the banks and the vaults — everything — dissolves into a great, featureless void. Nobody can exist there, and there is not even a hint of any kind of ground or atmosphere. Only one thing does not disappear here: the spark of self-consciousness." In an even lower purgatory, "a spark of consciousness flickers to the end, and the magnitude of its suffering surpasses even the imagination of the demons themselves."[12]

For Andreev, even in the most hellishly constricted dimensions, "a spark of consciousness" flickers. So it must: what could suffer if there were no consciousness? If liberation is the detachment of the *purusha* from its experience, hell consists of its becoming so inextricably enmeshed with its own experience that it seems to have no escape. This explains the colossal sense of stagnation that characterizes Andreev's Worlds of Retribution. Swedenborg's descriptions of hell give a similar impression.

We could multiply examples from the religious and mystical literature of the world. In sum, they all tell us that the plane of existence that we call physical reality is not the only plane there is. Far too much evidence has accrued over the centuries that tells us otherwise. The other planes, both higher and lower, seem to be characterized by the degree of identification between *purusha* and *prakriti*. The parameters in each particular realm are extremely narrow; to go past them is to move to another plane. Even according to Hinduism and Buddhism, which hold that liberation is possible in a human body (according to some, *only* in a human body), ultimate liberation, *moksha* or *parinirvana*, is usually said to come only at death.

All this said, we come to a question that is unusually hard to answer. Again it involves causation. Granting that these different planes of reality exist, what kind of connection do they have? Do they sit one atop the other, separate and detached, like a set of plates, or do they interpenetrate? If they do interpenetrate, do events in one level cause events in another?

These questions are of no relevance to materialism, which claims that there is only one plane of reality, but they are extremely important to the esoteric traditions, most of which do say that there is such an interchange. It is symbolized by Jacob's vision at Bethel: "And he dreamed, and behold a ladder set up on the earth, and the top of it reached to heaven: and behold the angels of God ascending and descending on it" (Genesis 28:12). To Kabbalists, the ascent and descent symbolize this interpenetration between worlds. Moreover, events on higher, subtler levels somehow cause those on lower levels, just as your mental conception of the cake you are about to bake precedes and causes the manifestation of the cake.

So it would seem, but is this right? Or are we merely dealing with a more specialized and intricate form of constant conjunction? Let's create two strings of digits:

3485980316089848959316205879542457932<i>1</i>...
5080908528321007471532765293000011359<i>0</i>...

These are similar to the strings we looked at in the previous chapter, except that now the sequence interlocks between two lines. Every time we have a 3 in the line above, there is a 5 in the line below. Are we justified in saying that the 3 in the line above somehow "caused" the 5 to appear in the line below? It would not seem so.

This kind of causal sequence is different from the one-dimensional material causation analyzed by Hume. It has to do, for example, with relations between strings of events in the psychological, or "astral," world and strings of events in the physical world. To take a simple example, say there is a seer who has prophetic dreams. Every time she dreams of a major airplane crash, such a crash occurs the next day. Even if the correlations between dreams and crashes were infallible, we still could not say that the dreams caused the crashes. All we could say would be that there is a correspondence between the two.

In all fairness, this is ultimately what the esoteric traditions are saying. They rarely speak of causation, but they frequently speak of correspondence. The most famous axiom is from the *Emerald Tablet* of Hermes Trismegistus: "What is above is like that which is below, and what is below is like that which is above" (usually elided to "As above, so below"). Antoine Faivre, the distinguished French scholar of esotericism, has even said that the doctrine of correspondences is one of the central elements of esotericism as a whole.

Probably the most famous instance of the doctrine of correspondences is astrology. Most scientists today treat astrology with contempt, but they forget that this ancient art was originally (and to a great extent still is) as empirical and inductive as science itself. It began with the Sumerians and Babylonians, who, after millennia of scrupulously recording the movements of the planets, came to see certain correlations between these movements and events on earth. (In those days natal astrology — reading the birth chart of an individual — had not been invented; the art was used to foretell the patterns of weather and the rise and fall of nations.) Certain planets, especially Jupiter and Venus, were correlated with luck; others, particularly Saturn and Mars, were equated with ill fortune.

Does astrology work? It works well enough. To take a fairly recent example, in the fall of 2000, astrologers could see that the U.S. elections were due to take place when the planet Mercury was moving retrograde. This usually indicates delay, confusion, and sometimes deceit, and few astrologers would advise anyone to make a major decision under its influence. The week before the election, I received emails from various astrologers suggesting that there would be some sort of problem with the electoral results, even accusations of fraud. The excruciating aftermath of the ballot proved them right. Even more peculiarly, Mercury was due to station (that is, stand still in the skies from the earth's point of view) and go direct around 9:45 PM on election day Eastern time. Watching the returns on television, I was struck by the fact that the networks took Florida, the crucial state, out of the Democratic column at almost exactly that time.

Astrology employs the doctrine of correspondences: there is a correlation between events on earth and those in heaven. Nevertheless, both types of events are physical: one type — the movements of the planets — is correlated to another — certain events on earth. Hence astrology is empirical and inductive. It has been discarded by science because the latter can find no causal mechanism that would explain the connection of planets and events on earth, but if Hume is right, *any* causal connection is merely one of conjunction. There is no a priori reason to discard astrology any more than there was to discard the theory of evolution in, say, 1870, before Mendelian genetics was devised to explain how traits are inherited. Practically the only man who tried to make a serious and objective scientific analysis of astrology, the French psychologist Michel Gauquelin, did find statistically significant correlations between the positions of planets in the natal chart and success in careers such as medicine and sports. Even though his findings did not entirely jibe with conventional astrology, the scientific community refused to accept Gauquelin's conclusions. Some scientists replicating his studies found that their results corroborated

Gauquelin's. Unable to accept this outcome, they falsified their own data.[13]

But even astrology does not require us to radically revise the notion of causation as I've set it out here. We notice sequences: certain events accompany or follow upon others; it remains a case of constant conjunction. These are all elements of experience; they are patterns in the garment of *prakriti.*

Other attempts to go past causation in this sense have met with no more success. The foremost of these is C. G. Jung's concept of "synchronicity," an "acausal connecting principle" that supposedly explains what Jung calls "meaningful coincidences." Jung describes a famous case in point:

> A young woman I was treating had, at a critical moment, a dream in which she was given a golden scarab. While she was telling me this dream I sat with my back to the closed window. Suddenly I heard a noise behind me, like a gentle tapping. I turned round and saw a flying insect knocking against the window-pane from outside. I opened the window and caught the creature in the air as it flew in. It was the nearest analogy to the golden scarab that one finds in our latitudes, a scarabeid beetle, the common rose-chafer (*Cetonia aurata*), which contrary to its usual habits had evidently felt an urge to get into a dark room at this particular moment. I must admit that nothing like it ever happened to me before or since, and that the dream of the patient has remained unique in my experience.[14]

Such events are common, and I could cite any number of examples of synchronistic occurrences from my own and from others' experiences. For Jung, synchronicity is the principle that connects two events that are themselves not causally related. Jung is not saying that the woman's narration of her dream caused the arrival of the beetle, or vice versa. But what he *is* saying is not altogether clear. Sometimes he implies that these events are unrelated and that the only connection they have is the meaning the individual ascribes to them. More often, he suggests that a certain hidden cause is responsible for both of these apparently coincidental occurrences. This cause is the archetypes — primary forces that underlie the human psyche, or, as Jung defines them, "formal factors responsible for the organization of unseen psychic processes," for example, dreams — and synchronistic occurrences. "Meaningful coincidences . . . seem to rest on an archetypal foundation," he writes.[15] Jung is saying, not that there is no causal connection between these events, but rather that the true cause for both is an unseen occult or psychic factor: the archetype.

Jung tries to avoid any causal implications of his theory: "As soon as [the observer] perceives the archetypal background he is tempted to trace the mutual assimilation of independent psychic and physical processes back to a (causal) effect of the archetype, and thus to overlook the fact that they are merely contingent. This danger is avoided if one regards synchronicity as a special instance of general acausal orderedness."[16] But his attempts are not altogether convincing. He seems to be saying that the archetype did not *cause* the events associated with it (for example, the dream of the scarab, the appearance of the beetle at the window), and that they are simply associated with it contingently. He appears to be assuming that all causal relations are necessary rather than contingent (that is, they *must* have caused their associated effects, rather than merely having *happened* to cause them), but this is not true. Many causal relations are purely contingent. A man's child leaves its toy on the stairs; the man trips on it and falls down. In this case the toy on the stairs caused the fall, but it was not strictly *necessary*: the man could have stumbled and fallen even had the toy not been there. Consequently the archetype could, in some sense, have caused the physical phenomena associated with it even if it did not do so necessarily.

It's easy to see why Jung was so evasive about this point. By the eighteenth century, science had drummed all occult causes out of its worldview, so, as a scientist, Jung could hardly be expected to embrace them. On the other hand, he was honest enough to grope with phenomena that reductionistic science did not acknowledge. As a result he was forced to create the theory of synchronicity, which is something of a halfway measure between occult philosophy and a modern rationalistic explanation.

I discuss synchronicity at such length because it is a word that is thrown about today though often poorly understood. But from the point of view of causation, as I have described it here, the outcome remains the same. Even if there is an archetypal cause that underlies these two apparently unconnected events, it is still a case of constant conjunction. The only real difference is that the archetype is never directly visible; it makes itself manifest only in its effects — in a dream or an intuition or the toss of some coins in a reading of the *I Ching*.

To sum up these insights, we could return to the helpful although simplistic metaphor of strings of digits. Let's say there is not one but many strings of digits, each of which represents a certain bandwidth of manifestation. If consciousness is able to step back — to detach itself — from these to some extent, it may well be able to correlate certain patterns in one string (for example, the psyche) with those of another (physical reality). This would go far toward explaining the apparently superhuman powers of telepathy and clairvoyance attributed to spiritual adepts. But this circumstance does not really force us to change the theory; it is still a matter of discerning patterns in the garment of *prakriti*.

At any rate, by this view no item in the pattern, strictly speaking, causes another, any more than the letter *i* in the word *it* causes the letter *t*. The cause is, as Jung intuited, hidden, but it may go deeper even than the archetypes. It may lie in this intricate dynamic between *purusha* and *prakriti*, between consciousness and experience, or (as the old occultists used to call them) spirit and matter. One element, certainly, is the degree of enmeshment between the two. How this comes about can be glimpsed, but it can only be glimpsed. As H. P. Blavatsky writes, "The 'Causes of Existence' mean not only the physical causes known to science, but the metaphysical causes, the chief of which is the desire to exist.... This desire for a sentient life shows itself in everything, from an atom to a sun.... According to esoteric teaching, the real cause of that supposed desire, and of all existence, remains forever hidden, and its first emanations are the most complete abstractions mind can conceive."[17]

A "sentient life" is impossible without sensation, and sensation is impossible without consciousness — the capacity to relate self and other. So the root of all existence is the primordial distinction between self and other. Blavatsky is right in saying that "the real cause of that supposed desire ... remains forever hidden." The Rig Veda implies as much at the end of its famous creation hymn: "Whence this creation has arisen — perhaps it formed itself, or perhaps it did not — the one who looks down on it, in the highest heaven, only he knows — or perhaps he does not know."[18]

For a taste of this mystery, simply close your eyes, calm your breathing, and try to still your mind. This will be next to impossible; thoughts and feelings will come up regardless. The calmer your mind is, the more disconnected and arbitrary will be the thoughts that arise. Images will appear out of nowhere, things you had long ignored or forgotten. If you are attentive, you will begin to notice a kind of blank space, a deep silence in the mind, out of which the thoughts arise. The most common name for this silence in Western esotericism is the Abyss. The Yogachara school of Buddhist philosophy has called it *alayavijnana* — "the ground of consciousness"; the equivalent term in Tibetan is *kun gzhi*. The Tibetans also call it *ma rigpa* — the primordial loss of awareness that gives rise to all phenomena.

Could it be that, contrary to all I've said up to now, it is in this dark space of being, this space between thoughts, that God inserts himself into the chain of causation? It is possible, maybe probable. But if so, it is very far from causation in any accepted scientific or theological sense.

In any case, it's paradoxical that what we call consciousness should arise out of a primordial loss of consciousness, and I must admit that it is a mystery I don't fully understand. Maybe it's foolish to believe that you can understand it if, as the Rig Veda says, even the supreme deity may not understand it either. Nor for that matter do we remember the moment of our conception. There is something in our origins that remains, and perhaps must remain, veiled from our sight.

CHAPTER SIX

A JUST UNIVERSE?

In chapter 1, I mentioned a study of comparative attitudes toward fairness in humans and in our close relatives the chimpanzees. The study showed that a chimp will take a bad deal, because anything is better than nothing, whereas a human will not. A human will walk away from an unfair deal even if he goes away empty-handed.

The implications of this study may be more far-reaching than they appear. What if a human were to take this stance toward that most treacherous of all deals, which is life itself? Other animals accept what life dishes out; they will fight to stay alive no matter what. Humans don't behave the same way, at least not always. There are those who decide to walk away from what they perceive as the unfair deal of life. This would explain why humans sometimes commit suicide, while chimps don't.

Suicide, like so many things in human behavior, transgresses the limits of what is natural. If life, stripped down to its core, is pure survival, what are we to say of someone who doesn't want to

survive? While there are extreme circumstances that would justify such an act — those of individuals who have painful terminal
illnesses, or of concentration camp internees who make a desperate run for it — most suicides don't take place in such situations.
Nor is it always a matter of privation. In the United States as of
2008, the general suicide rate was about 11 per 100,000. Among
middle-aged white women, the rate was 8.2 per 100,000; for black
women in the same age group, the rate was only 2.5 per 100,000.[1]
If suicide were entirely, or even mostly, due to hardship, one might
imagine that the rate of suicide among black women, whose
poverty level is much higher, would also be higher, whereas the
opposite is the case.

No doubt there are clinical reasons for suicide — depression
and so on — but sometimes assigning such a label looks like an
instance of the naming fallacy: slapping a label onto something in
order to pretend you have understood it. What if, for many people, the root lies deeper? What if it is a way of stepping away from
a deal they don't think is fair?

A research psychologist could probably find a way of testing
this hypothesis ("of 100 individuals who attempted suicides, 45
agreed with the statement 'Life is unfair,' as opposed to the control
group, of which only. . ." and so on), but as I'm not a research psychologist, this is not a direction I will take. Instead I'm led to reflect
on the extremely powerful need in the human soul for justice —
and justice, moreover, in the universe as a whole, not merely in
human society. Without this sense of justice, it is difficult to see
meaning or purpose in life.

Granted, it's not always easy to believe in the fundamental justice of the cosmic order. The Japanese director Akira Kurosawa
titled an early film of his *The Bad Sleep Well*, and often this seems
to be true. In fact it's extremely hard to believe in the justice of

the cosmos if we take life at face value. The wicked prosper, the good suffer; "the race is not to the swift, nor the battle to the strong" (Ecclesiastes 9:11). Hence people have resorted to many explanations, particularly religious ones, to balance the accounts.

One of the most far-reaching attempts to create a theodicy (a theory of divine justice) came from the Hebrew prophets in the eighth to sixth centuries BC. Its context was God's covenant with Israel. The conditions were clear: "And it shall come to pass, if thou shalt hearken diligently unto the voice of the Lord thy God, to observe and to do all his commandments which I command thee this day, that the Lord thy God will set thee on high above all nations of the earth: And all these blessings shall come on thee, and overtake thee, if thou shalt hearken unto the voice of the Lord thy God. . . . But it shall come to pass, if thou wilt not hearken unto the voice of the Lord thy God, to observe to do all his commandments and his statutes which I command thee this day; that all these curses shall come upon thee, and overtake thee" (Deuteronomy 28:1–2, 15). A long list of afflictions follows.

The nation did not meet the requirements, and the afflictions came. The prophets had no doubt about who was responsible. Isaiah declaimed, "Through the wrath of the Lord of hosts is the land darkened, and the people shall be as the fuel of the fire" (Isaiah 9:19). By that time Israel was divided into two kingdoms. The northern kingdom, known simply as Israel, was destroyed by the Assyrians in 722 BC. The people, deported en masse, vanished from history (hence the Ten Lost Tribes of Israel). The southern kingdom of Judah was crushed by the Neo-Babylonian empire under Nebuchadnezzar in 587 BC, the Temple of Solomon was sacked, and the people were removed to Babylon. This time they did not lose their identity but nursed hope of a return to their home. This hope came to fruition: after Babylon was in its turn overthrown by the Medes and Persians, their king, Cyrus, issued an order in 539 BC stating that the people of Judah — the Jews — could return and rebuild their temple.

In a sense, all was well again, and the Jews enjoyed almost four hundred years of peace under the Persians and their heirs, the Hellenistic monarchs. And yet a nagging doubt remained: did the people's sins really warrant such terrible afflictions? The second part of the book of Isaiah (generally dated to the time of Cyrus's restoration) hints at this question: "Comfort ye, comfort ye, my people; speak ye comfortably to Jerusalem, and cry unto her, that her warfare is accomplished, that her iniquity is pardoned: for she hath received of the Lord's hand *double* for all her sins" (Isaiah 40:1–2; my emphasis). Somehow the punishment seemed out of proportion to the crime.

The most famous of all inquiries into divine justice is also dated to this era. The story of Job is too well known to rehearse here, but we can see that the dramatic, as well as the theological, tension in the book comes from one underlying question: why should the righteous suffer? Job, from the land of Uz (probably in today's Jordan), is a Gentile, so he is out of the range of Israel's retributions. After the long interchange between Job and his so-called comforters, which occupies the greatest part of the book, the Lord himself appears out of the storm cloud to answer (if it can be called answering): "Where wast thou when I laid the foundations of the earth? . . . Who hath laid the measures thereof, if thou knowest?" (Job 38:4–5).

Some commentators, notably Jung in his *Answer to Job*, have seen the divine response as a show of force: the Lord displays his overwhelming power and Job must submit. But, like most interpreters, I think the text's real import lies elsewhere. It is a question not of superior force but of superior understanding. "My thoughts are not your thoughts, neither are your ways my ways, saith the Lord" (Isaiah 55:8). Divine justice is not commensurable with human justice.

Even so, there is a rough correlation between the two. Having received "from the Lord's hand" double for all their sins, the Jews return to Jerusalem. Job, yielding in humility, has his goods and chattel restored to him; new children are born to replace the ones who were killed. But after the number of sins has been tallied up against the number of retributions, we are still left with a remainder, and it has nagged at the part of the human mind that will not submit to an unfair deal. Do the sins really match the punishment? Does Job's new set of children wipe out the memories of those he has lost? Is justice dealt out fully in earthly life?

The answer of the Hebrew prophets was eschatological. Justice will be accomplished in the end — but only in the end. At that point, the prophets foretold, the Lord himself will stand against the wicked and set the whole world right: "And the Lord shall be king over all the earth: in that day shall there be one Lord, and his name one" (Zechariah 14:9).

It would be hard to overstate the influence of this answer. Every signboard worn by every street-corner fanatic, every fraudulent bestseller proclaiming the end of the "late, great planet Earth," every convoluted calculation demonstrating when the Lord shall return is a direct descendant of this prophetic vision. They are all, in effect, delivering the same message: divine justice does not manifest fully in the world we know; the world will have to come to an end to set the accounts straight. To this day, the half of the human race that adheres to one of the Abrahamic faiths accepts some version of this belief.

Yet its grip is weakening. It is hard to believe in imminent apocalypse when we know that the earth was not created in

4004 BC but is billions of years old. It is hard to believe the prophets when prophets have been crying wolf for the past twenty-five hundred years. The strident and vicious apocalyptic preaching of recent years sounds more like a death rattle than the voice of resurgence.

Even if the prophecies come true, we could wonder how a Last Judgment really could set everything right. Would it repay humanity for all its sufferings? Many of these, it is true, have been inflicted by humans on other humans, but at least as many — disease, starvation, earthquakes, storms — have been wrought by the impersonal hand of nature. I'm reminded of a science-fiction story (I don't know the author's name) in which Jesus Christ returns at the Last Day only to find the planet empty. Delving into a vault in the earth, he finds a sign that reads: "We were here. Where were you?"

Blasphemous, perhaps, but still a haunting statement. Even Christianity has not felt satisfied with a theodicy that depends entirely on the Last Judgment. In addition to this "general judgment," as theologians call it, there is the "particular judgment" that takes place upon the death of each individual and will determine whether she is sent to heaven or hell. These two judgments have never entirely jibed: why should everybody have to be judged twice? The answer, in historical terms at any rate, probably has to do with the hybrid origins of Christianity: it took the apocalyptic vision of a Last Judgment from its Jewish roots, and the heaven and hell of an afterlife from Greek and Egyptian mystery religions, and has attempted to paper over the inconsistency with theologizing.

Setting aside this issue, we can ask whether the afterlife of conventional Christianity will satisfy our hunger for a righteous universe. The obvious answer is no: what sort of justice sentences a person to an infinity of torments in hell for a finite number of offenses in a lifetime? Even the greatest monsters of history did not inflict an infinite amount of damage in the few short decades of their lives.

There is no good answer to this question. It may be true that God's ways are not our ways, but aren't God's ways supposed to be better than ours? Eternal torment in hell is not the work of an infinitely loving God; it is the work of a God who is tremendously more vindictive than the typical human being. Theologians usually reply by murmuring something about the need to balance divine love with divine justice, or the extent of the punishment having to do with the infinitude of the one offended. Here is one version, by the twentieth-century theologian Reinhold Niebuhr:

> The classical Christian idea of Atonement emphasizes that God is both the propitiator and the propitiated. The Father sends the Son into the world to become a sacrifice for sin. But it is also the wrath of the Father which must be propitiated. There can be no simple abrogation of the wrath of God by the mercy of God. The wrath of God is the world in its essential structure reacting against the sinful corruptions of that structure. . . . The mercy of God represents the ultimate freedom of God above His own law; but not the freedom to abrogate the law.[2]

You could turn this passage into an atheist's jibe: can God make a law so powerful that he can't abrogate it?

One alternative admits the existence of heavens and hells but does not portray them as infinite. This is the standard doctrine of Buddhism, which says that the six *lokas* of existence constitute a cycle. As monumental as the sufferings of the hell realms are, they do come to an end. By accumulating good karma, beings climb up the ladder of these realms until they reach the heavens of the gods, who are immeasurably long-lived by human standards but not immortal. When their merit has been exhausted, these beings fall back into the hell realms to start the cycle all over, and so it will continue unless they are freed by enlightenment. The wheel is endless, and we have all followed it from beginning to end in an uncountable series of recurrences. Each of us has been a god, each of us has been in hell countless times. The thirteenth-century Tibetan sage Longchenpa writes:

> All the tears you have shed would be more (than the water) in
> the four oceans,
> And the amount of molten metal, foul blood, and excrements
> You have consumed when your mind had become a denizen of
> hell or a spirit
> Would not be matched by the rivers flowing to the end of the
> world.[3]

Similarly, Andreev's Worlds of Retribution are not endless; even the Torquemadas will eventually work off the evil they have done.

The only major figure in Christian theology to have embraced a theory like this was the church father Origen (circa 185 to circa 253), who held that "the soul-like condition comes from the angelic and archangelic condition, and the daemonic and human from the soul-like; and that conversely from the human come angels and daemons, and that each order of the heavenly powers is made up either wholly of those below or from those above, or else both from those above and those below."[4] Here we see something like the Buddhist doctrine. Being a Christian, however, Origen did not see the cycle as endless. Instead he believed that all beings would be reconciled to God in the end; even the devil had the chance of being saved.

The Origen passage that I've quoted, incidentally, does not necessarily consist of Origen's own words. It is taken from an anathema issued by the Second Council of Constantinople in 553, which, three hundred years after his death, denounced Origen's teaching about the preexistence of souls. The wording may or may not be Origen's exactly, but scholars believe that it accurately represents his doctrine. In any event, the anathema itself reveals how this teaching fared in Christian dogma.

Because Origen's concept of the preexistence of souls is sometimes taken as equivalent to that of reincarnation or transmigration, I should say something here about the place of this teaching in Christian doctrine. Many New Age writers say that reincarnation was taught in early Christianity and was suppressed only later by one or another church council. Origen is sometimes held up as an early champion of reincarnation. But he did not teach the idea of reincarnation or transmigration; in fact he opposed it: "The doctrine of transmigration . . . is foreign to the Church of God, and not handed down by the apostles, nor anywhere set forth in the scriptures."[5] Nor did any of the other church fathers embrace reincarnation. Some have speculated that the doctrine did exist in early Christianity, and probably it did in certain Gnostic sects; but to all appearances, it has never had a place in the protocatholic church or its descendants, Catholicism, Orthodoxy, and Protestantism. The reason is summed up by the Franciscan Pat McCloskey on his website: "Reincarnation denies the need to convert, about which Jesus spoke often. If souls keep recycling, won't they all end up in the same place eventually? If so, why are our decisions today important?"[6]

Nonetheless, the church's rejection of a doctrine does not make it untrue. Nor is it a convincing argument to deny a teaching just because it might lead some to put their salvation off till the next life. Many American Catholics apparently agree: a Harris poll taken in November 2007 indicated that about 24 percent of them believe in reincarnation (a slightly higher percentage than that of the populace at large, which is 21 percent).[7]

In fact an enormous amount of material indicates that there is some truth to the doctrine of reincarnation. The late Ian Stevenson, who headed the department of psychiatry at the University of Virginia, did extensive research on past-life memories and published his findings in four volumes titled *Cases of the Reincarnation Type*. The Jungian psychologist Roger Woolger, author of *Other Lives, Other Selves*, has built a worldwide practice on healing individuals from past-life traumas. These findings are empirical, even if they are of the anecdotal type that quantitative analysts treat with such contempt. But if we are going to be truly and rigorously empirical, we must consider the full body of evidence and not just the small quantity that can be classified as repeatable results. Anyway, what sort of experiment could you devise that would indicate anything about the afterlife one way or the other?

We could say the same about life after death as a whole. A tremendous body of firsthand experience points toward the survival of consciousness after the body's demise. When I was editor of *Gnosis*, a journal of the Western spiritual traditions, I received quantities of first-person accounts by ordinary people of encounters with dead relatives, angels, and other spiritual entities. *Gnosis* did not publish this type of story, but people sent them anyway, to the point where I came to regard them as a nuisance. Most were believable; often they were written by people who previously had had no interest in religion or the paranormal. Furthermore, there was a sharp line separating this material from intricate paranoid fantasies, crudely scrawled missives by the Supreme Being, and other offerings that were clearly insane. (We received our share of these as well. Jay Kinney, founder of the magazine, created a "nut drawer" to preserve the wildest of them.)

Well, then, which is it? Heaven and hell or reincarnation? There is no reason to embrace one exclusively at the expense of the other. Let me go back to a model I mentioned in the previous chapter, in which the many levels of existence are differentiated by one variable: the degree to which *purusha* is enmeshed with *prakriti*. Each plane is defined by a specific degree of this admixture (though this is almost certainly impossible to define in quantitative terms). If this is correct, then upon death an entity could move to a "higher" or "lower" level or, alternatively, could remain on the same plane for another life, depending on any number of factors. One of these is likely what Emanuel Swedenborg called your "ruling love." According to Swedenborg, your condition in the afterlife is not based on the record of your sins as interpreted by Saint Peter, or on the weight of your heart on the scales of justice, as the ancient Egyptians believed. You go where you will in the next life on the basis of your affinities. "*We are our love and intention after death*," writes Swedenborg. "All heaven is differentiated into communities on the basis of differences in the quality of love, and every spirit who is raised up into heaven and becomes an angel is taken to the community where her or his love is. . . . The same applies in hell. There too, people associate according to loves that oppose heavenly ones."[8]

C. S. Lewis, in his allegory *The Great Divorce*, suggested something similar: The communication lines between hell and heaven are open all the time; anyone in hell can go to heaven anytime he wishes. But those who are in hell do not like heaven and do not feel comfortable there; the very blades of grass cut their feet.

From all this, we can begin to tease out a picture of the afterlife that is both reasonable and concordant with justice as we understand it. There are "many mansions," as Christ said, encompassing levels of reality that stretch beyond the vision of even the minc's eye. We go where we go after we die not after some ruling by a celestial criminal justice system; rather it is a question of where we want to be. Or, to put it in a more sophisticated way, the *purusha* in us — that fragment of the cosmic Self that animates our being, that is our being — is drawn to the realms with which it has the most affinity.

The Eastern traditions do not speak of ruling loves or affinities they characterize the fate of the soul in terms of karma. Karma — from a Sanskrit root meaning "to act" — has a number of meanings in the East, and it has become a popular word in the West as well. My friends in San Francisco used to say someone had "parking karma" if she was good at finding spaces for her car in that notoriously congested city. There it seemed to mean "good karma," probably from an unconscious association with the English word *charm*. But the most universal sense of the word — and the one that concerns us most here — is as defined by the Indian scholar Pandit Rajmani Tigunait:

> Each school of Indian philosophy accepts the immutable law of karma, which states that for every effect there is a cause, and for every action there is a reaction. A man performs his actions and receives remuneration for them. If he becomes attached to the results of his actions, then he becomes a victim of his own karmas because it is attachment to the results, or fruits, that then motivates or conditions a person to perform future actions. The fruit has arisen out of the action, and the action out of the fruit. This cycle is referred to as the wheel of karma. To act with the motive of gaining fruits invites bondage, but to relinquish this motivation frees one from all miseries. All schools of Indian philosophy agree that this concept of karma is the only satisfactory explanation for the existence of suffering. The apparent good fortune of nonvirtuous people and bad fortune of virtuous people can be explained only through the law of karma, which

explains the reason and purpose for a person's existence in his present life. According to this law, nothing is accidental; whatever happens in one's life is because of karmas performed in this life or in a past life.[9]

Most discussions of Indian religion define karma more or less this way. (By the way, when Tigunait speaks of "all schools of Indian philosophy," he is including Buddhism as well as the Hindu schools, since Buddhism originated in India, even though it's no longer practiced widely there.) Compared to the standard Christian view, in which the wildly disparate fortunes of individuals on earth can only be ascribed to the capricious will of God (since the soul did not exist before birth and so could not have done anything good or bad), it is at least a rational account of the good and evil that comes to us in life. Moreover, it appears just: you are repaid for an action in proportion to the benefit or harm you have caused. Not surprisingly, it accords well with the Samkhya philosophy. Attachment, as Tigunait calls it, is precisely the entangling of consciousness in its contents, of ensnaring *purusha* in *prakriti*. The remedy is to perform one's actions dispassionately and without expectation of results. The divine Krishna gives similar advice in the Bhagavad Gita: "When all a man's emprises are free from desire [for fruit] and motive, his works are burnt up in wisdom's fire, then wise men call him learned. When he has cast off all attachment to the fruits of works, ever content, on none dependent, though he embarks on work [himself], in fact he does no work at all."[10] The Sanskrit word here translated as "work" is *karma*, so the last line is also saying, "He generates no karma at all."

Nevertheless, the justice of karma is almost as problematic as that of conventional Christianity. Suppose that around the year 1500 an inquisitor in Spain ferrets out dozens of Jews for torture. He dies in old age, not only unpunished but honored by his church and country. Four hundred years later, that same inquisitor is reborn as a Jew in Poland. When the nation is conquered by the Nazis, he is shipped off to Auschwitz and is exterminated after suffering unimaginable agonies. The inexorable law of karma has been served. But is it just? The Jew has no memories of his previous life as an inquisitor; he dies in despair at the injustice of the world, utterly unaware that he has brought this fate upon himself by his own evil karma. It would be as if the state were to sweep a man off the street one day and execute him for a murder without bothering to tell him why. In fact it's worse, because the murderer might at least have some inkling of why his fate has befallen him, whereas the Jew in Auschwitz has none.

In all fairness, the proponents of the law of karma are not exactly saying that it is just; they are simply saying that one thing leads to another. By its logic, the Jew in the case I've described could be reborn in the next life with karmic dispositions toward persecution as a result of the traumas of the concentration camp, and the whole process could start all over again. In fact, that's what's likely to happen, and that's why Tigunait can speak of the "cycle" or "wheel of karma." The remedy is not virtuous acts in themselves, because these will simply create good karma. This will bring good fortune to an individual, but once the karma is exhausted, he will have to pick up where he left off. The true solution is virtuous acts performed selflessly and dispassionately, without attachment to results.

I have more to say later about the connection between virtue and liberation, but for now let's go back to another point that Tigunait makes in the passage quoted. The law of karma "states that for every effect there is a cause, and for every action there is a reaction." Most definitions of karma make mention of cause and effect, and sometimes karma is even defined simply as the law of cause and effect. This can be confusing for Westerners, whose view of causality probably resembles those I discussed in chapter 4. But there is a crucial difference. Karmic causation makes no sense unless we grant one supposition: that *similar causes have similar effects*. The Western view makes no such presuppositions; it is completely empirical. Concerned only with discovering which kinds of effects are conjoined with which causes, it does not presuppose whether the cause is "like" its effect.

It's striking that the spiritual traditions of India should have portrayed the moral structure of the universe in such a deterministic way, but it makes sense if we look at the situation more closely. For Hinduism and Buddhism, unlike orthodox Christianity, the Absolute is impersonal. Although it may take the form of personal gods (even a singular, quasi-monotheistic God known as Ishwara), these are merely guises for something that can never be constrained by any form, no matter how overweening. Relying much less on a personal God to enforce cosmic justice, these traditions have a greater need to portray this justice in the form of deterministic law. By contrast, the West, which has always had its God in the background to say, "Vengeance is mine; I will repay" (Romans 12:19), has not needed to impart this function to causality. Consequently it has had more liberty to look for empirical results as they are, instead of adopting a preconceived notion of what they should be. It would be fascinating to see whether the concept of karmic causality in Hindu and Buddhist philosophy impeded the advance of empirical science in those civilizations, but I suspect this would take a lifetime's study.

The law of karma is problematic in other ways as well. If there is no conscious connection between the persecuting inquisitor and his later incarnation, the persecuted Jew, who or what exactly is carrying the karma? The problem is heightened for Buddhism.

Based on the doctrine of *anatta*, or "no-self," Buddhism claims that the very notion of a self is delusory. *Anatta* literally means "no atman." Here Buddhism diverges from Hinduism, which teaches the existence of the transcendent Self known as atman, or *purusha*. At bottom this often seems to be the only real difference between Hinduism and Buddhism at all.

Buddhist answers to the conundrum of what carries karma are often vague. The typical answer is by analogy to waves that follow one upon another in the ocean. There is no connection between the waves; one simply gives rise to another through a sort of inertia. But applied to the survival of consciousness after death, this analogy is not very illuminating or even accurate. After all, the waves presuppose the existence of the ocean, but it is the very existence of this ocean that the Buddhists deny.

Not all Buddhists deny the existence of a self or "I" completely, at least in a relative sense. The Dalai Lama observes, "There is indeed a conventionally posited, valid I — a self that is the doer of action, that is the accumulator of karma, and that is the person undergoing the pleasure and pain that are the fruit of those actions. However, when we examine the mode of apprehension of the mind when the I becomes a troublemaker, we find that we are conceiving a self-instituting I that is an exaggeration beyond what actually exists."[11]

He goes on to give a standard Buddhist proof: this "I" is dependent on "the aggregates of mind or body." That is, if you take apart the bundles of your sensations, thoughts, emotions, and so on — and much Buddhist meditation is designed to do exactly this — you will find nothing there behind them, no "I" that is real or substantial. Logically, this is fallacious. You can disassemble your automobile into an "aggregate" of parts and supplies, but it does not follow from this that there is no automobile at all.

Moreover, the automobile in its fully constructed form is something beyond what its parts would be if they were just piled up in your driveway. So it is with the "I." The fact that it can be dissected does not prove there was nothing to dissect.

Ultimately the Hindu doctrine of atman, or Self, and the Buddhist doctrine of *anatta*, or no-self, may not be nearly as far apart as their names imply. In fact these apparently opposite terms may refer to the same thing. The Chinese Buddhist master Hui-neng says, "The Buddha-nature knows neither decrease nor increase, whether it is in the Buddha or in common mortals. When it is within the passions, it is not defiled; when it is meditated upon, it does not become purer. It is neither annihilated nor abiding; it neither comes nor departs; it neither dies nor is born. It remains the same all the time, unchanged in all its changes. As it is never born, it never dies."[12]

Compare this to the description of the Self in the Hindu Brihadaranyaka Upanishad:

> [Atman, or Self,] is neither big nor little, neither long nor short, neither burning like fire nor flowing like water; without shadow, without darkness, without wind, without air, without attachment; without touch, taste, sight, smell; without hearing, speaking, thinking; without breath, without face, without energy, without measure, without inside or outside; it consumes nothing; nothing consumes it. . . .
>
> Who without knowing this Root, meditates, sacrifices, practises austerity, though for thousands of years, does what passes away. Who dies without knowing this Root, is pitiful; who leaves this world, knowing it, is wise.[13]

The principle of which these two passages speak appears to be the same, whether we call it atman or *anatta*, Self or no-self. It is Self in that this principle of consciousness constitutes the very core of our being. It is no-self in the sense that it far surpasses the very limited sense of self with which we usually identify.

Something similar is true when we look at the "accumulator of karma," which in many Hindu schools is *ahamkara*, or ego. Most Buddhist traditions do not give it a specific name, since that would suggest it is "real," but as we've seen from the Dalai Lama's remarks, the concept is somewhere in the background. In any event, *purusha*, the true Self, and *ahamkara* (to use the Samkhya terms) are very much distinct. The first is consciousness in a pure, unbounded form; the second is consciousness that has fixated on its experience, on its own contents, and imprisons itself by calling them *mine*. This very fixation is the glue that attaches *ahamkara* to the fruits of its action.

In the end, karma is a shadowy entity. Sometimes it appears to work; sometimes it does not; sometimes it is instantaneous; sometimes it takes centuries to fulfill itself. If there is cosmic justice in this process, it is impossible for a human being to understand, much less rely on. Moreover, we have always been told — and rightly — that to be good out of fear of punishment is a low motivation. This must hold true whether we are afraid of the policeman or of the machinery of karma. If there is a moral component to the universe, it has to run deeper than this.

And it does. To best approach it, we can turn back to a detail that I mentioned in a previous chapter. The Samkhya says that *purusha* is manifold, that there are many *purushas* rather than just one. The proof is factual: if *purusha* is singular and one individual attains enlightenment, wouldn't that mean that everyone else automatically would as well? A singular *purusha* would mean that either everyone has attained enlightenment or nobody has.

The French esotericist René Guénon, whose understanding of Hindu thought was more lucid and profound than that of practically anyone else in the West, makes this reply: *purusha* is "a multiple principle only so long as it is considered in relation to separate existences."[14] *Purusha* is only *relatively* multiple; it is so on our plane of reality but not on all. Taking this a step further, we could say that *purusha* is plural only insofar as it is fixated on *ahamkara*, on the ego. In fact it is this very sense of the multiplicity of *purushas* — the apparently rigid division between self and other, or between *selves* and *others* — that binds us most rigidly to this plane.

The solution, of course, is to let these barriers drop. Meditation, again, has been proposed as a means to this end, but meditation alone can become somewhat solipsistic. The boundaries of identity have to be loosened in other ways as well, and the most powerful way to do this is by ethics in its deepest sense.

The self as an ego is separate and isolated. Trafficking in debts and obligations and duties and karma, it operates by a kind of double-entry accounting system: assets must balance out liabilities, whether we are thinking in terms of torts and crimes or of giving Christmas gifts. This is no doubt necessary in ordinary human society, but at bottom it seems cold and calculating. We distrust others when we find them acting this way, and when we find ourselves acting this way, we feel ashamed. This is because intuitively we know there is something deeper going on, even if we're unaware of it consciously. In my *Conscious Love* I call this "transactional love." Nearly everything we call love in this world is of this kind.

It can be depressing to think of love this way, and this is largely because we know love should be something more. It is this higher love, which Christianity calls *agape* and I call "conscious love," that reflects the insight that the Self at the center of one's own being is exactly the same as the Self that lies at the core of everyone else's as well, human and nonhuman, animate and apparently inanimate. Christ commands us to love our neighbors as ourselves because our neighbors literally are ourselves.

I won't develop this line of thought further because I've done so at great length in *Conscious Love*. But even the small amount I've said here shows how neatly and fully the project of kindness and compassion dovetails with that of individual liberation. The entire history of Buddhism reflects this. Originally, liberation was for the individual: "Work out your salvation with diligence," said the Buddha on his deathbed. This idea is still the core of the Theravada branch of Buddhism. Five hundred years later, the message began to change with the advent of Mahayana, the "Great Vehicle" of Buddhism, which teaches that liberation for oneself alone is incomplete. The true saint, or bodhisattva, renounces his ascent to nirvana until all sentient beings are liberated as well.

This too looks merely like a high-minded sentiment until we see that it reflects the truth about the universe. *Purusha* is one, so none are truly liberated until all are liberated. We are to love our neighbors as ourselves not because God will punish us otherwise but because the bond that links all of us is violated when hatred and harm are present. There are many good souls who grasp this truth intuitively and act according to it without understanding why, but there are others, those who want to *know*, who need to grasp it with their minds as well as their hearts. And until both mind and heart do grasp it, our minds will be restless and our hearts unsatisfied.

CHAPTER SEVEN

BEYOND THE COPPER MOUNTAIN
The Dimensions of Faith

The Sufis, the mystics of Islam, tell a story about three men who have heard of a mountain of gold that lies in a remote country. The men decide to make a journey to find it. They go for a very long way, and have almost given up hope, when they reach a mountain of copper. They debate among themselves about whether the legend misled them and was really speaking of this copper mountain. Finally one of them says, "Well, in any case, copper is quite valuable. I could mine this copper and become rich." So this man stays at the copper mountain, and the other two go on.

They journey for a long way — two or three times the distance they covered to reach the copper mountain — and they have almost given up hope when they come to a silver mountain. Again, the two men ask themselves whether this was really what the legend was talking about when it spoke of a mountain of gold. One of them says, "In any case, silver is extremely valuable. I could mine this silver and become rich." He stays behind, leaving only one of the original three to go on.

The last man has to travel a very long time — three or even four times as long as it took to reach the silver mountain, and often he curses himself for not having the sense to have stayed behind with his fellows. But he goes on until all his supplies are gone and he has nothing left. He is almost dead of starvation when he finally spies the mountain of gold.

Why does one man stop at one point, and why does another go on? Should the two men who stopped have gone on to their original goal? Why, for that matter, did they start on the journey? What were they really seeking? And why did they believe the legend to begin with?

One thing this parable is talking about is faith. It is hard to go far in thinking about religion without coming up against this monumentally difficult subject. What I have said so far in this book requires little faith in order to be accepted. But it's a different matter when we take up the issue of a personal God. Since such a God is invisible and apparently imperceptible in the world as we know it, faith suddenly becomes vitally important — except, it seems, no one can quite agree about what this faith is or what it should be based on. Immediately we find ourselves floating on a sea of discord, and like squabbling sailors on a sinking ship, we discover that our divisions only make things worse.

To speak of faith is to invoke Christianity, because no other religion in the world has placed such emphasis on faith or made so many demands on it. However post-Christian our civilization may be at this point, if we bring our thoughts to bear on faith, we will probably do so in terms of Christian concepts and categories. So it's worth devoting some attention to these.

Probably the oldest form is _faith through authority_. You believe because someone or something you look up to — your church, scripture, master, tradition — tells you to. Leslie D. Weatherhead, a British Methodist minister writing in the 1960s, gives an example in his provocatively titled book *The Christian Agnostic*.

> A Methodist youth had fallen in love with a Roman Catholic girl, and as his parents disapproved of such a marriage, he wrote a naïve letter asking me if I would interview them both and, to use his own words, "convert the girl to Methodism"! I was happy to interview them both to see what would happen. That girl had been well instructed. Whenever she was confronted with a difficult situation, she fell back on the phrase, "Well, our church teaches so and so." In effect, she said to me this: "Who am I, a young, uninstructed, uneducated girl, to decide what is to be believed? For hundreds of years the great theologians, the great scholars of my church, adequately educated and magnificently equipped, have wrestled with these problems and come to certain conclusions. I, an untrained girl, can only accept what they say. I believe in what my church teaches." As Dr. Vincent Taylor [another Methodist minister] once said, "No wonder Rome makes converts. It is all so simple once we have committed mental suicide by agreeing that the church cannot err."[1]

It's tempting to dismiss the girl's ingenuousness until we realize that we do the same thing all the time. There are any number of areas in which we have no competency to make decisions and have to trust experts. If your washing machine breaks and the repairman comes to fix it, you put your faith in what he tells you about how it is to be fixed. If you fall ill, you go to the doctor and (usually) trust her diagnosis. Why should we imagine that the situation should be different with religion, where the evidence is all the more ambiguous and the difficulties all the more subtle?

Nevertheless, faith in authority has diminished enormously over recent centuries. It was easier, no doubt, to maintain it in medieval Europe, when there was one church in which all spiritual authority was concentrated. It is not so easy today, when there are countless religions, each of which constantly insists the others are wrong.

Furthermore, we live in an age of suspicion. We find it hard to naively assume that the authorities are making their pronouncements solely with our benefit in mind. This distrust pervades most fields of human life. More and more often we view our leaders as mere politicians who are eager to lie for the slightest advantage, our doctors as minions of the obscenely profitable pharmaceutical industry, and the very journalists who bring us news of these things as flunkies of the rich and powerful. Religious authority, for a large segment of the population, evokes at least as much distrust. Some of it may be misplaced or exaggerated, but in any case the spell has been broken. We now feel cut adrift, forced to rely on our own judgment, but free to make our own mistakes.

The second type of faith is the _faith of reason_. Here you believe because you have been rationally persuaded to do so. This is faith as known through the theological and philosophical proofs and refutations — the ontological argument, the argument from design, and so on. Anyone who has read an elementary textbook of philosophy is familiar with these strategies. Unfortunately they have not worn well over time. *apologetics*

The ontological argument, for example, devised by the medieval theologian Anselm of Canterbury, states that, since God is defined as the best and greatest being one can imagine, God must necessarily exist. It is clearly better, Anselm contends, to exist than not to exist, so a nonexistent God would _not_, by definition, be the best and greatest being imaginable. Hence God necessarily exists. Although Anselm's proof has been much admired for its ingenuity, it has not convinced most philosophers. They recognize that the argument involves a circularity, even though the exact nature of this circularity has been notoriously hard to pinpoint.

The argument from design has fared no better, even though it has been recently resurrected under the name "intelligent design." It's becoming easier and easier all the time to understand the order of the universe without having to invoke a conscious, personal designer who created this order; like Laplace, science has no need of that hypothesis.

That reason is not necessarily the smoothest path to faith has long been acknowledged, and Christianity from its earliest times has invoked the opposite: *faith through absurdity*. Paul set the tone:

> For the preaching of the cross is to them that perish foolishness; but unto us which are saved it is the power of God.
>
> For it is written, I will destroy the wisdom of the wise, and will bring to nothing the understanding of the prudent.
>
> Where is the wise? where is the scribe? where is the disputer of this world? hath not God made foolish the wisdom of this world?
>
> For after that in the wisdom of God the world by wisdom knew not God, it pleased God by the foolishness of preaching to save them that believe. (1 Corinthians 1:18–21)

There is a strange beauty in these paradoxes, which speak to the part of the mind that realizes the world is not all that reason makes it out to be. Whether Paul meant to take his point further than this is not clear; at any rate, later Christian apologists certainly did. We have already encountered Tertullian's "Prorsus credibile est, quia ineptum est" — usually rendered as "Credo quia absurdum": "I believe because it is absurd."

The ultimate step toward absurdity was taken by the Danish philosopher Søren Kierkegaard in the nineteenth century. In his journal he writes, "The believer, therefore, is the man of character, who, in absolute obedience to God, regards it as a duty not to want to understand." And: "All this world history and the reasons and proofs for the truth of Christianity must be suppressed. There is only one proof, one alone: that of faith."[2] At times Kierkegaard sounds like the girl in Weatherhead's story. It's not surprising that his critics have sometimes accused him of verging on Catholicism.

Kierkegaard's most famous treatment of faith is his *Fear and Trembling*, which focuses on Abraham's sacrifice, or near sacrifice, of his son Isaac on Mount Moriah (Genesis 22:1–15). Abraham "believed by virtue of the absurd, for human calculation was out of the question, and it was indeed absurd that God, who demanded [the sacrifice] of him, in the next instant would revoke the demand," Kierkegaard writes. He goes on to say that "the movement of faith must constantly made by virtue of the absurd."[3] For Kierkegaard, faith is faith precisely *because* it is absurd. (His use of this word deliberately invokes the formula "Credo quia absurdum.") If it weren't, faith would simply be rational knowledge.[4]

This argument proves something, but possibly not what Kierkegaard intended. Let's grant that we are to believe in the absurd. Which absurdity, then, shall we choose? There's virtually an infinite quantity to pick from. Kierkegaard, trained as a Lutheran divine, was bound to see it in Christian terms. What impels us toward faith to begin with is the pervasive notion of sin. Here is another passage from Kierkegaard's journal: "There is only one proof for the truth of Christianity, and that is precisely the pathological proof: when the anguish of sin and the pangs of his conscience force a man to cross the narrow dividing line which separates the despair bordering on madness and . . . Christianity. There lies Christianity."[5]

This may have had some force in Kierkegaard's time, when a pervasive notion of sin — especially original sin — had saturated the mental atmosphere precisely through the influence of Christianity. Paul claimed that this knowledge of sin had come through

Jewish law: "I had not known sin, but by the law" (Romans 7:7). The pathological "anguish of sin" was, however, the creation not of Judaism or its law but of Paul and his Christianity. Paul proposes Christ as the remedy for this pervasive sense of sin that, it would seem, he himself has invented. It is as if a man were to go to a doctor who told him he had some disease that the doctor himself had thought up — for which, of course, only the doctor could have the cure. Could orthodox Christianity, starting with Paul, have created this pathological sense of sin so that it could proffer itself as the remedy?

All of this leaves us wondering which absurdity we should believe in. Perhaps, as Kierkegaard thought, the naked condition of man in a state of sin before God. Or perhaps, as the existentialists would later claim, the exact opposite: the naked condition of man alone in a universe *without* God. Kierkegaard, the devout if tormented Christian, is often seen as the first existentialist. It's odd that his ornate chain of paradoxes, strung together to lead toward faith, should have helped create a philosophical school that has been among the most relentlessly atheistic of all time. It would appear that one's choice of absurdities is a matter of taste.

In the end, then, faith by virtue of the absurd must take its place alongside the other rational or quasi-rational arguments, which are plausible to the exact degree that one is disposed to believe them at the outset.

This issue leads us to what may be the central type of faith, at least in its conventional form — volitional faith. Here one believes as a matter of will, maybe even of choice. Kierkegaard has sometimes been classed among theologians who hold to this view, although he probably did not. In his *Philosophical Fragments*, he writes, "It is easy to see . . . that faith is not [merely] an act of will: for all human volition has its capacity within this scope of an underlying condition. . . . If I do not have the condition[,] . . . all my willing is of no avail."[6] That is, you can believe all you like, but if there is no underlying reality to correspond to your belief, it is "of no avail."

A purer form of volitional faith is offered by the great American psychologist and philosopher <u>William James</u>. In his 1896 lecture "The Will to Believe," James argues that in situations where you can't find certitude, it is not only your privilege but your duty to choose on pragmatic grounds: <u>you choose the system of beliefs that makes your life better and more complete.</u>

> In truths dependent on personal action, . . . faith based on desire is certainly a lawful and possibly an indispensable thing. . . . To preach scepticism to us as a duty until "sufficient evidence" for religion be found, is tantamount therefore to telling us, when in presence of the religious hypothesis, that to yield to our fear of its being error is wiser and better than to yield to our hope that it may be true. . . . Dupery for dupery, what proof is there that dupery through hope is so much worse than dupery through fear?

James goes on to say that "we have the right to believe at our own risk any hypothesis that is live enough to tempt our will."[7] As extreme as this may sound, James makes it clear that he is talking about assertions — such as the existence of God — for which the evidence is equivocal. In these cases, why *not* let your desire choose? Unfortunately James seems to assume that your level of knowledge will remain static: if you can't make a determination about the truth of faith at one point, you will never be able to. Therefore you might as well make your decision now. This is not a terribly comforting position. What if new information comes along that challenges your belief? In many areas of life, it's acceptable and even desirable to change your position as new knowledge is presented, but it is awkward in the realm of faith, which, as the theologian Paul Tillich observed, has to do with matters of "ultimate concern."[8] You can change your mind about computer brands or presidential candidates with some equanimity, but if your "ultimate concern" slips away from you, you are lost. As Schopenhauer writes, "Actually it would be a bad business if the principal thing in a man's life, his ethical worth that counts for eternity, depended on something whose attainment was so very much subject to chance as are dogmas, religious teachings, and philosophical arguments."[9]

The various strategies for justifying faith — rational, emotional, volitional — all run aground on the same shoal: the stupendous human capacity for self-deceit. None of these approaches can stand against the mind's own power to lead itself astray — not merely to be mistaken but to *want* to be mistaken. James is right to say that negative dupery is no better than positive dupery and very likely worse, but is there any way we can hope not to be duped at all?

HIS WAY OUT

As far as I can see, there is only one way out. The Epistle to the Hebrews alludes to it in a famous verse: "Now faith is the substance of things hoped for; the evidence of things not seen" (Hebrews 11:1). This is a paradoxical utterance, rather like Kierkegaard's clever extravagances, although much more profound. Faith is both substance and evidence; that is, it has a palpable aspect, even though (as the verse also makes clear), it is not palpable in the ordinary sense of the term. Nevertheless, in some way and at some level, faith must be based on experience. A person who has faith does so not because of authority or reason or desire but because, however obscurely, he senses an unseen reality that is drawing him in its direction. This is the only way that faith can be immune to self-delusion.

The rest of Hebrews 11 gives a list of Old Testament exemplars of faith. The passage is a piece of magnificent sermonizing and has inspired quantities of magnificent sermonizing in the millennia since it was written, but its argument seems strangely beside the point today. The figures that the author* sets before us are indeed a lofty set — Abel; Enoch, the antediluvian patriarch who walked with God; Noah; Abraham; Sarah, who "received strength to conceive seed." Noah was "warned of God of things not seen as yet"; Abraham was called "to go out into a place which he should receive for an inheritance"; Sarah "was delivered of a child when she was past age, because she judged him faithful who had promised" (Hebrews 11:7, 8, 11).

These figures, as presented by the epistle, differ from us in one crucial respect. They had faith in the promises made by God. But in order to hear these promises, they had to have some experience of God, and that is what a person who faces the question of faith today probably lacks. A modern person might object that she might well believe in God's promises if God himself appeared to make them. Indeed that is the vital question now: not whether God's promises come true, but whether a God capable of making such pledges exists in the first place.

The author of Hebrews seems aware of this problem: "He that cometh to God must believe that he is, and that he is a rewarder of them that diligently seek him" (Hebrews 11:5). But the Old Testament exemplars did not have to take that first step: they didn't have to "believe that he is" — that he exists. All of them had direct communication from God almost as a thing taken for granted. Of course I'm not claiming that the biblical stories are factually true

---

* The epistle is traditionally attributed to Paul, but very few scholars today believe he wrote it; various candidates have been suggested, but none have won general acceptance, so it's best to regard the author as anonymous.

in any sense by which we would normally understand those words. But even taken as mere types of faith, their example is wanting.

Well, then, are we merely to sit stupidly in front of the television before God takes the trouble to appear in the living room? Of course not. The real answer to the question of faith lies in the opening verse of this chapter of Hebrews, which does express a powerful truth. There is "evidence of things not seen" and a "substance of things hoped for." In terms of the story of the golden mountain, it is that dim yet compelling intuition that leads a man to go out of his house and travel on an endless journey.

In his book *The Sovereign Soul: Sufism, a Path for Today*, Phillip Gowins, a contemporary Sufi teacher, describes his own spiritual awakening:

> One night when I was twenty-six, I was lying in bed next to my wife (my first wife, I mean), waiting to fall asleep, when a sensation like a traveling electric shock swept down through my body.
>
> I thought nothing of it until it happened again. It happened a third time, then kept on happening at three- or four-second intervals. It was like a pulsing hoop of energy that started at my head and coursed down through my entire body — like a wave front hitting the beach again and again.
>
> I was puzzled, then alarmed, then frightened, then finally scared, until I was begging it to stop. But it just went on and on. It seemed to be happening on some psychic level, maybe in my aura (though I didn't know what an aura was then), and despite my pleading I remember thinking that it was really all right, that no actual harm was being done to me. And then, just when I thought it was over, another wave came crashing down, exploding, enlivening, energizing me. Then it stopped.

The next morning Gowins saw nothing new in himself, "only the same old frightened loser who looked back from the mirror at me every day." On the surface, nothing changed in his life. He continues:

> The next stage in my spiritual odyssey (though I didn't yet know that I was on one) took place when I was sitting in a state of reverie on the living room floor of our house in Oregon (I may have been stoned), gazing out the window at a very tall, very green pine tree. I was thinking about how the world was a big objective whole and not just the series of disconnected perceptions we all have of it. This way of looking at things may be very familiar to some, but it was new to me, and I was much enamored of it. It had also dawned on me that this objective whole might be a conscious, living entity — alive like myself — and that if I wanted to be of use to this dynamic, living world, then I should seriously dedicate myself to being a conscious, aware part of its single-entity aliveness.
>
> And then, suddenly, I took a vow to whatever cosmic forces rule. I vowed that whatever I could do or however those forces could use me to be of service to the world, I would be at their disposal.
>
> This was something that came from so deep inside me that it surprised even me. But I knew I truly meant it.

Gowins's life then fell apart. His wife left him, taking their children with her, and he ended up living in a spare room in his brother's house. He spent a couple of years drifting, idly looking at the occasional book on meditation or spirituality. It was only when he chanced to attend a lecture by the Sufi teacher Pir Vilayat Inayat Khan that he came to see his true path. "When I caught my first glimpse of Pir Vilayat, I knew I had come home."[10]

The point is, of course, not that Sufism is the true path for everyone — Gowins emphasizes this point repeatedly in his book. It's simply that the path took this form for this particular man.

Here is another example, from a very different figure: Maximilian Kolbe, a Polish priest who died in Auschwitz and was later canonized by the Catholic Church. One night when he was young, after being scolded by his mother, he recollected, "I asked the Mother of God what was to become of me. Then she came to me holding two crowns, one white, the other red. She asked me if I was willing to accept either of these crowns. The white one meant that I should persevere in purity, and the red that I should become a martyr. I said that I would accept them both."[11]

On the face of it, these two accounts could hardly be more different. One is from a Catholic saint, the other from a self-described "frightened loser." One is laden with theological content; the other is virtually devoid of any such thing. One involves some very specific — and excruciatingly stiff — requirements; the other entails nothing more than an apparently vague wish. And yet if we go past the level of the obvious, we can see their essential similarity. Both are grounded first and foremost in *experience*. No one is signing articles of faith or marching to the podium at the end of some evangelical entertainment. It is only out of experience that commitment arises.

It would be easy to multiply other such cases; the mystical literature is full of them. But are these experiences free from the risk of self-deceit?

This question takes us to the arcane philosophical issue of how mystical experience is to be understood. Hard-bitten scoffers write it off as fantasy or delusion. Not long ago it was even fashionable among psychologists to attempt to diagnose the pathologies of specific mystics: Teresa of Avila was nothing more than a hysteric, Joan of Arc a schizophrenic.[12] But the typical schizophrenic can barely keep her own life together; she is not likely to arise out of total obscurity and drive an army of powerful invaders from her land. Hysterics (or what used to be called hysterics) do not found great monastic orders or write spiritual classics. Consequently this approach explains nothing.

A more subtle attempt at discrediting mystical experience lies in what is called the contextualist view. Contextualism arose in reaction to the thought of philosophers of religion — William James the foremost among them, although a similar view was expressed more recently by W. T. Stace in his *Mysticism and Philosophy* — that some essential mystical experience is universal and ultimately, as James put it, "ineffable." This latter view is often called essentialism.

By contrast, contextualism argues that very little, if anything, is genuinely universal in mystical experience; rather, it is heavily conditioned by the culture and religion in which it takes place. The most prominent advocate of this perspective is a contemporary philosopher named Steven T. Katz. In one essay he writes regarding mystical experiences in the Kabbalah: "The entire life of the Jewish mystic is permeated from childhood up by images, concepts, symbols, ideological values, and ritual behaviour which there is no reason to believe he leaves behind in his experience. Rather, these images, beliefs, symbols, and rituals define, *in advance*, what the experience *he wants to have*, and which he then does have, will be like." After going on to evaluate mysticism in other religions, Katz concludes, "Our investigation suggests what it suggests — a wide variety of mystical experiences which are, at least in respect of some determinative aspects, ideologically grounded."[13]

Certainly Katz is right to a degree. After all, it is a rare Muslim who has a vision of the Buddha, and the Catholic Maximilian Kolbe saw the Virgin Mary rather than Parvati or Kwan Yin. But contextualism runs the risk of simplistically concluding that mystical experience is totally preprogrammed: you see what you expect to see and there is nothing more to it than that. This is not entirely true, as we see from the case of Phillip Gowins. His experience was not culturally determined; he was not looking for anything and did not have the words or concepts to define what he felt. It may be that if he had been raised in the atmosphere of a particular faith, his experience would have taken that form, but he wasn't and it didn't.

The same holds true even more powerfully for those experiences that directly counter what an individual might have expected or wanted. These are reasonably common; we've already seen A. J. Ayer's encounter with the red light in chapter 1. For a far better-known example, we can turn to the most famous mystical experience in all of Western history: Paul's conversion on the road to Damascus (Acts 9:1–9). Because Paul himself says he had this experience (see 1 Corinthians 15:3–9), we can't write it off as a quasi-mythical element later tacked on to the story of his life. But the whole point of this experience — where he is confronted by a vision of the risen Christ, who asks, "Saul, Saul, why persecutest thou me?" — is that it overturns his previous perspective. It is the opposite of being "ideologically grounded."

For a contemporary example, there is the weird story in Howard Storm's *My Descent into Death.* The author tells of how he fell dangerously ill during a trip to Paris and lapsed into a coma. He had a harrowing near-death experience in which he was being carried off by demons until he was somehow able to jabber a nonsensical prayer cobbled together from a few scraps of religious-sounding phrases he had learned in his childhood, including the Twenty-third Psalm, "The Star-Spangled Banner," and the Pledge of Allegiance. At this point Christ appeared, drove the demons away, and showed Storm a vision of heaven. By Storm's own account, he was an avowed atheist before this time, so again his ideological grounding would have been weak or nonexistent.

There is a delicate balance to be struck between contextualism and essentialism. Spiritual experience is universal and displays many common features (for James, they included such characteristics as ineffability and a "noetic quality") across different cultures.[14] At the same time, those who have these experiences strongly tend to express — and even perceive — them in terms of more or less familiar images. This seems to be a deeply rooted tendency in the human mind: to clothe new experiences in the forms and structures of old or familiar ones. For Howard Storm, who was raised in a Christian culture, his sojourn in the afterlife took the form of seeing demons and being rescued by Jesus. A Tibetan might see the manifestations of wrathful deities instead of demons, and Chenrezig (the Tibetan god of compassion) instead of Christ. Xenophanes, a Greek philosopher of the sixth century BC, put the point strongly: "But if cattle and horses or lions had hands, or were able to draw with their hands and do the works that men can do, horses would draw the forms of the gods like horses, and cattle like cattle, and they would make their bodies such as they had themselves."[15]

But, you may reply, isn't this what contextualism is claiming? Not quite. The contextualists often seem to be saying that most or all of religious experience is a matter of self-suggestion, of "cupery," to use James's word. But actually it seems that there is genuine religious experience, and even that it is universal or practically so, but that the mind will process and describe it in different ways depending on the mind's conditioning.

An example from a different arena may illustrate what I'm trying to say. All human beings with normal vision see the same range of the color spectrum, but the terms in which these experiences are expressed may be quite different. Languages with comparatively rich color vocabularies (such as English) divide the spectrum into narrow bandwidths, each with its own name; consequently, in the blue-green range, we may distinguish teal from aqua from turquoise. Languages with fewer color terms tend to break the spectrum into broader bands. Ancient Greek, for example, was comparatively poor in words for colors. Hence Xenophanes (whose views on anthropomorphism we've just encountered) could break the rainbow down into three colors: purple, red, and yellow-green.[16] *Ios* was black, blue-black, or purple. "Yellow-green," *chloros*, had to do for covering the range of the colors that we break up into green and yellow. Reading Homer, you can come across an apparent reference to "green honey." Did the Greeks have green honey? Almost certainly not. (Something being called green honey was sold recently in the Philippines, but this turned out to be sugar syrup with food coloring added.)[17] The poet probably meant to speak of what we would express as "yellow honey."[18] And Xenophanes may have actually seen three colors in the rainbow where we might see seven or more. Nevertheless, these differences have not led even the most merciless skeptics to assert that the experience of light or color is delusory.

Something similar may be going on with the images that clothe religious experience. The experience is not self-delusion, but it tends to be cast in language and images familiar to the person in question. A mystical experience of compassion may be personified in the mind of one individual as Avalokiteshvara or Kwan Yin, in another as the Virgin Mary.

It has been proved over and over again: the human mind processes its experiences in certain patterns and structures — Kant's categories. All the same, the mind is experiencing *something*: the world is not the dream of a solipsist. How and whether we can isolate what used to be called "raw sense-data" from the process of interpretation and categorization will be a subject for debate for a long time to come. But this does not entitle us to conclude that the mind's experience is total dupery. This is true whether we are talking about the color spectrum or manifestations of the divine.

All this said, let's look now at how the divine actually manifests itself and what clue these manifestations give to its nature. To return to the primordial duality I've been exploring in this book, there is that which *experiences* and that which *is experienced*: "I" and the world, *purusha* and *prakriti*. The divine can manifest in either or both of these guises. How it does will determine its appearance and even its apparent location.

Let's begin with the divine as it manifests in that which experiences. Clearly if we are going to have any sense of this, we must turn to that which experiences in us, that which says "I." We will also have to take this "I" in a wider and more comprehensive sense than we usually do. To many people, the "I" is indeed God. But it is the "I" of the ego, the personal self, their own wishes and desires and urges. It is an unstable entity: suspicious, fearful, obsessed with dangers (usually imagined), status, power, and so on. The ego is not God in any ultimate sense, but it can act as if it is. It then becomes, in the language of Christ's parable, the steward who oppresses the other servants in the master's absence (Matthew 24:45–51).

But then there is the master himself or herself — the "true I," the Self that is beyond the level of worldly preoccupation. This Self — which is emphatically *not* the lower self or the ego — is at the core of our being. It is not, strictly speaking, God, but it is the place in us where we connect with God. It is the immanent God: "And they shall call his name Emmanuel, which being interpreted is, God with us" (Matthew 1:24; compare Isaiah 7:14). This true "I" — the consciousness that looks out at the world through each of us as through so many windows — has many names. Esoteric Christianity calls it the Son; the Logos; Sophia, or "wisdom"; or the kingdom of heaven. For the Hindus it is atman; the Dzogchen tradition of Tibetan Buddhism speaks of it as *rigpa*, "pure consciousness"; other Buddhists call it "Buddha nature" or simply "mind." You can never see it, because it is that which sees. Francis of Assisi alluded to this when he said, "What we are looking for is what is looking."

The most explicit equation of this "I," or true Self, with God appears in the Advaita Vedanta, and most people who have read something of this tradition will find this concept familiar. Sri Ramana Maharshi was once asked if God is personal. He replied, "Yes, He is always the first person, the I, ever standing before you. Because you give precedence to worldly things, God appears to have receded into the background. If you give up all else and seek Him alone, He will remain as the 'I,' the Self."[19] Another twentieth-century Advaita master, Sri Nisargadatta Maharaj, says, "My state is: I am, without parents. I am the Unborn. Similarly, I understand you as such only. You are also the Unborn, without parents."[20]

As I've stated both here and elsewhere in my works, this teaching is implicit, and sometimes explicit, in esoteric Christianity, and the words of Christ ultimately do not make a great deal of sense without it. At the same time, *exoteric* Christianity has been excruciatingly uncomfortable with such concepts and has backed away whenever it has come close to them. At one point Sri Ramana Maharshi was interviewed by a French Jesuit. The priest asked him, "I come from God. Isn't God distinct from me?"

Ramana Maharshi replied, "Who asks this question? God does

not. You do. So find who you are and then you may find out whether God is distinct from you."

"God is infinite and I am finite," said the Jesuit. "I have a personality that can never merge into God. Isn't that so?"

"Infinity and perfection do not admit of parts," said Ramana Maharshi. "If a finite being is apart from Infinity, the perfection of Infinity is marred. Thus your statement is a contradiction in terms."

The conversation ended inconclusively, with the Jesuit abruptly leaving to catch a train.[21] But the entire interchange reflects the deep divide between those who say that ultimately God and the Self are one, and those who say that the chasm between the two can never be bridged. Conventional Christianity has almost always insisted on the latter claim.

Christianity is not the only monotheistic religion to emphasize this point. In the world of Islam, the ninth-century Sufi mystic Mansur al-Hallaj said, "I have seen my Lord with the eye of my heart, and I said: 'Who are You?' He said, 'You.'" Al-Hallaj's most famous utterance was "Ana'l-haqq": "I am the Truth."[22] Since *al-haqq*, "the Truth," is one of the traditional ninety-nine names of Allah, this statement was denounced as blasphemy. Al-Hallaj was arrested, imprisoned, and finally executed by the caliph of Baghdad in AD 922.

Why should these traditions insist so vehemently on the radical and unbridgeable gap between God and man? Certainly there is some danger in equating the "I" with God. To say "I am God" or "I am the Truth" with the petty egotistic self in mind (consciously or unconsciously) is to fall into one of the most dangerous of all spiritual traps.

Nonetheless, we may wonder if the authorities are insisting on this radical cleavage between the divine and the human entirely with our best interests in mind. If we are ultimately one with God, then this unity is our inalienable birthright, and religion exists only as a midwife to higher realization; no authority has the right to insert itself between us and our deepest essence. But this is precisely what religion has so frequently tried to do — with remarkable success. One of its most common strategies has been to insert a set of propositions — doctrines and dogmas — between the individual and God: you must first believe certain things about God or you will not be allowed access to him. Of course Christian apologists have frequently said that faith is far more than mere assent to a set of propositions, and they are right. But somehow assenting to those propositions is always part of the process, and it is not optional.

Consider this case. A man, confronted by existential anguish, cries out from the depths of his soul to God. And God answers. The man feels the answer in as palpable and profound a way as he felt the doubt, and he comes to have faith. To reinforce it, he turns to religion. Soon he learns that religion orders him to believe in a whole set of dogmas that make no sense to him rationally or emotionally, but which he is told he must believe in order that his faith might not be in vain. For a while he forces himself to accept these, but sooner or later he sees that they are nonsense. He casts off the dogmas and the religion, but at the same time he comes to discount the profound experience of the divine that had originally impelled him to believe. And the last state of that man is worse than the first.

This is a composite case. It is the story of no one, and it is the story of dozens of people I have met and dozens more that I have read about. It's so common that, when I meet someone new and begin to discuss spirituality with him or her, I can almost always expect to hear some variant of it.

Conventional religion provides comfort and guidance for

hundreds of millions of people, and there is no reason to denounce it wholesale. But for those who want something deeper, it may be possible to go back to the primordial dichotomy that I have been exploring in this book. God is *purusha*, Self, that which *sees*; it is that which is most profoundly and intimately "I." God is also *other*, *prakriti*, the "world," that which *is seen*. How the divine is revealed is a matter, almost, of the stance from which we see it. Even Ramana Maharshi did not wholly repudiate the personal God, as we see in this reply to one devotee who claimed to be a sinner:

> Why do you say you are a sinner? Faith in God is enough to save you from rebirth. Cast all your burden on Him. In the *Tiruvachakam* it is said: "Though I am worse than a dog, You have graciously undertaken to protect me. The delusion of death and birth is maintained by You. Is it for me to sit and judge? Am I the Lord here? Almighty God, it is for You to roll me through many bodies, or keep me fixed at Your feet." Therefore have faith and this will save you.[23]

Consequently we see a dual perspective even in the purest forms of nondualism. God is both wholly Self and wholly other. To put it more comprehensively still, God is the ultimate source out of which this duality of self and other arises.[24] There are times when, in moments of rare clarity, you can perceive the pure mind of divine consciousness peering out at the world through your own limited vessel; there are also times when you feel helplessly isolated from this consciousness, when it is perceived as wholly other, and you are left with no alternative other than to "cast all your burden on Him." The focus shifts along with the arbitrary tides of mood and circumstance, but there are any number of ways of viewing and experiencing this reality, and there is always farther to go. The golden mountain itself may not be the final destination.

CHAPTER EIGHT

THE CONSCIOUS CIVILIZATION

As I think about the implications of the ideas in the previous chapters, I'm struck by the traps that lie in wait. Among the most pernicious is the temptation to sound the call for a new religion. A streamlined Samkhya, say, where people go to services to hear readings from the *Samkhyakarika*, with a giant mural of Shiva and Parvati in the background, and have intense theological discussions about the singularity versus the multiplicity of *purusha* and other such matters.

One could do this. Marketed the right way, it could prove lucrative for New Age entrepreneurs, a crowd that seems to be doubling every week. Many people have grasped the truth of L. Ron Hubbard's dictum that, in order to make a lot of money, all you have to do is start your own religion (which he proved by creating the Church of Scientology). But given the discord that each new religion provokes, at this point anyone who tries to add another to the list probably does not have humanity's best interests in mind.

And yet while the demise of the old faiths is predicted as frequently as the second coming of Christ himself, they will be with us for the foreseeable future. For this reason, it makes sense to ask how religions can move beyond the stockades of their own peculiar revelations without invalidating or diluting themselves.

One of the principal dynamics, as we've seen in the previous chapter, is between the personal and the impersonal God. To paint a picture with an extremely broad brush, the Eastern traditions have always stressed the ultimate impersonality of the divine, while the Western, Abrahamic faiths — particularly Christianity — have insisted on God's ultimate personhood. To the Christian, states of nonpersonal illumination or transcendence as experienced by the mystics of Asia are treacherous detours or, at best, mere way stations on the path to the personal God who has revealed himself in Jesus Christ. Conversely, to the Asian, the personal God is only a way station to the ultimate impersonal truth.

It's unwise to rush to any hasty conclusions about this point, or to smugly assume that "my" religion has the truth and all others are false or at best incomplete. Sooner or later such an approach ends in people breaking one another's heads, as Gurdjieff once remarked. In the end, we will have to see the fundamental truth of all perspectives, each in its own place.

In sum, this means that the divine is beyond all concepts and images. Practically all traditions admit as much. But they are rarely willing to admit that *their own* concepts and images are useful only insofar as they provide access to a higher reality. If they refuse to take this step, they bring to mind Christ's statement "Woe unto you, scribes and Pharisees, hypocrites! for ye shut up the kingdom of heaven against men: for ye neither go in yourselves, neither suffer ye them that are entering to go in" (Matthew 23:13). Most religions ask humility of their followers, sometimes to the point of self-abasement, but humility is a virtue that practically none of these religions have as institutions. It may be time they acquired it.

What this will mean for Hinduism and Buddhism is not clear to me (since I'm only distantly familiar with their day-to-day practices). For Christianity, it will probably mean granting what it has never wanted to grant: that the revelation of God through Jesus Christ is true and valid but not the sole or final or possibly even the most complete revelation of God to man. Still more importantly, Christianity will have to acknowledge that God is wholly self as well as wholly other, and that external forms of faith — including faith in Jesus Christ — are useful only as preliminary steps to this realization.

"No man cometh unto the Father, but by me," Jesus says in the Gospel of John (John 14:6) — a verse that has probably caused as much harm as any in the Bible. My own view of this statement, as with all the "I am" statements made by Jesus in this enigmatic text, is that it refers not to Jesus the man but, esoterically, to that which says "I am" in us, which is ultimately the true Self, *purusha*, or atman. The Father, then, would be that which lies beyond even *purusha*, beyond even the Self — in Hindu terminology, Brahman as opposed to atman. "I and my Father are one," says Jesus (John 10:30): as the Hindus say, Brahman is atman. And yet Jesus also says, "my Father is greater than I" (John 14:28). The Father — Brahman, the transcendent God — is greater than the Son — atman, the immanent God.[1]

Christ says, "I am the door" in the same esoteric sense (John 10:9). But the fact that "I am" is the doorway to God is something that Christian theologians have not wanted to touch. Consider this verse: "The kingdom of God is within you" (Luke 17:21). So reads the King James Version, which, for all its faults, in many ways remains the most intellectually honest of all biblical translations: the translators did their best to render what they thought the text actually said rather than what they thought it ought to say. Most modern versions are more disingenuous, and this verse is a case in point. The Revised Standard Version reads, "The kingdom of God is in the midst of you." The New Jerusalem Bible has: "The kingdom of heaven is among you." The New English Bible says, "The kingdom of God is in your midst." But the Greek reads *entòs humôn*, which literally means "within you," as the King James Version has it. The Greek word *entós* never means "among" or "in the midst of ";[2] other prepositions, such as *en* or *pará*, would have been used had that been its meaning.

This may seem like a pedantic point, but it shows up mainstream Christianity's discomfort with the idea of the God within. Yet the divine is, as we've seen, both wholly self and wholly other; by emphasizing the second at the expense of the first, Christianity has misled people not only theologically but also psychologically. For many, it has barred the gateway to their own "I."

Philip Pullman's fantasy novel *The Golden Compass* takes place in an alternate reality in which the soul of a human being takes the form of a "daemon," an animal with a palpable physical existence. A person is never separated from his or her daemon. But one character, the sinister Mrs. Coulter, is connected with a scheme to kidnap children and, by means of some advanced technical device, sever their daemons from them. (The closest analogy in our world would be a lobotomy.) The children subjected to this procedure are little more than walking shells. In the novel, to sever someone from her daemon is a crime beyond all imagining, but it provides an apt metaphor for what much of Christianity has been doing to its adherents for centuries. No wonder the visceral hatred for Christianity in the West seems to grow stronger every year.

It's obvious why Christianity has taken the position it has. Insisting more than any other religion on the personhood of God, it has constantly avoided anything that might imply that the individual Self could be merged into the greater, collective Self that is "God with us." (Mystics who have said otherwise, such as Meister Eckhart in fourteenth-century Germany, have usually fallen afoul of the authorities.) But this is an incomplete and distorted teaching, and it has caused untold damage. Kept ignorant of and isolated from the deepest layers of the Self, most people were docile adherents of the church for many centuries, but in recent generations they have fallen prey to anything that lays claim to authority: fascism, communism, fundamentalism, even a mindless and compulsive commercialism that has ravaged our souls and our civilization as well.

And yet to realize the Self, to know this "I am" that is the gateway to *purusha* if not *purusha* itself, is not an easy task. Most people are not interested in it. They think this is all very abstract and metaphysical and removed from their day-to-day concerns. But how can your "I," your own very essence, be removed and abstract?

These considerations raise the problem of esotericism in the true sense: dealing with a type of knowledge that is not for everyone because not everyone wants it. A brutally egalitarian American culture will call such a stance elitist, and so it has to be. But it's not a matter of a socioeconomic or even educational elite. (Most of my old friends from Harvard and Oxford have little interest in these subjects, and when I'm socializing with them, I usually find it more enjoyable to talk about something else.) The esoteric elite consists of those who want to know the truth and are not afraid to throw away their preconceptions — even those about their own nature and identity — for its sake. The people I've known of this type come from any number of backgrounds and social classes; some are well educated by conventional standards, some are not.

All this granted, who will decide who is to have access to this knowledge? For the individual, it's a process of self-selection. You stroll through a bookshop. On its shelves are romance novels, volumes of low-fat recipes, and guides on how to snare that special someone, as well as books containing the immeasurable wisdom of the ages. Which one attracts you says something about who and where you are. While sometimes a person has the sense of being tapped on the shoulder by a higher power and pushed toward a particular book or teaching or teacher, this is not decided by ordinary human criteria.

For the individual seeker, this simply means that you need to remain open to guidance and intuition as you find it. For religious authorities, the matter is not so clear-cut. The problem is compounded by the fact that most of these authorities — clergy, theologians, and so on — have no more sense of higher realities (and sometimes less) than the people they are supposed to lead. In the language of the Gospel, they "neither go in themselves, neither suffer them that are entering to go in." If religion is to continue as anything more than a mere simulacrum, it must be guided by those who are willing to "go in themselves," by those who are at least comparatively awake, rather than by those who are merely well trained in theological jargon. I can't predict the future of Christianity or any other religion, but I believe that it will belong to those faiths that are most truly committed to connecting people with this "I am," with *purusha*, rather than displacing it onto some external object or person, no matter how apparently holy.

For the religion of the third millennium, the task is to acknowledge that the barrier between God and Self is not sharp or rigid: that which says "I" in us is the very point at which we connect with the larger reality of the divine. This may be why the Gospels call it the "kingdom of God." In the language of the Samkhya, *ahamkara*, egohood, is the gateway to *purusha*, to the spark of consciousness that sits at the center of our being like a jewel in a lotus. (Like all gates, it can either let us in or keep us out.) The otherness of God, which Christianity has harped on for so long, must be met with the equally valid truth of the immanence of God — not as a spook hovering around in the atmosphere, but as the very consciousness that perceives at all. As *A Course in Miracles*, one of the greatest spiritual texts of the twentieth century, puts it, "God is the Mind with which I think."[3]

How institutional religion will accomplish this task is not for me to say. Instead let me turn to the institution that, far more than any religion, is regarded as the central authority of our time. Anything that wants to be taken seriously in our age must confront the edifice of science. Science is the great myth of our time, in both senses of the word: like the myths of the great world religions that preceded it, it provides a background of meaning for a civilization; and also like the myths of the world religions, its claims will, I suspect, ultimately be found to be not entirely true in an objective sense. But this discovery probably won't occur within our lifetimes.

As I stressed in chapter 1, I'm highly skeptical of today's innumerable attempts at reconciling science and religion, whether these take the form of "intelligent design," Zens and Taos of physics, or the nebulous entities that are touted as quantum spiritualities. These are intellectual gimmicks. At their best, they stimulate the creative imagination of both the scientist and the philosopher, but finally they will prove to be dead ends. The reason ought to be obvious: metaphysics is not physics; *metaphysics* literally means "beyond physics."* Sometimes it refers to esoteric philosophy (as you see when you go to a bookstore and pass an aisle marked "New Age; Metaphysical"), sometimes to the deeper questions of existence as conventional philosophy has tried to address them. Both forms have very little connection with science. Even so, there ought to be some meeting ground where science and metaphysics can sniff each other out. I think it's possible to sketch out how this might occur.

To begin with, why should there be many things rather than only one? As we've seen, the world arises when a self perceives an other, just as an infant begins to become conscious by distinguishing what is self versus what is not. If there is no self and no other, there is no world. At the same time this primordial distinction is only apparently true. *Purusha* experiences *prakriti*; *purusha* is conscious, *prakriti* is not. This would imply that in this process there is something that is not conscious: that which is experienced. But this is only apparently the case (hence, perhaps, the Vedanta's insistence that the world is *maya*). There is no place where consciousness is not present; one entity does not vacate the premises occupied by the other. As difficult as this may be to grasp, it has

---

* The genesis of the word *metaphysics* is peculiar. It originally derived from the title of Aristotle's *Metaphysics*. Practically all his surviving works consist of lecture notes edited by his pupils after his death. Organizing this collection, they put his treatments of such things as being and existence (subjects that Aristotle himself called "first philosophy," "theology," or sometimes "wisdom") after his *Physics*: hence they called this collection *tà metà tà physikà biblía*, or "the books after the *Physics*." *Physics, tà physiká*, means "things that have to do with nature." The Greek preposition *metá* can mean both "after" and "beyond," so in medieval times, "metaphysics" came to mean "that which lies beyond nature." See *The Encyclopedia of Philosophy*, ed. Paul Edwards (New York: Macmillan, 1967), 5:289.

important consequences. There is a self perceiving an other; but all the while the other remains conscious too. Therefore the first self becomes an *other* to the second self; it is not a static relationship but a dynamic interchange. In the language of the twentieth-century philosopher Martin Buber, we may think of the other as an "it," but it is really a "thou." Or we may go a step further and say with Freud, "Wo Es war, soll Ich werden": "Where *It* was, there shall *I* be."[4]

Suddenly, instead of one self and one other, we have two of each. But the process does not stop there. To perceive anything, as Heidegger understood, is to pick it out of a background; this is the root meaning of the word *logos*, which has had such a rich and compromised history in Western thought.[5] So now the self has not only one *other* to perceive but also a second one, the background. It's like the drawing of the optical illusion in which a vase can also look like a pair of silhouetted faces, depending on which you see as figure and which as ground. Hence there are two *others*. But the second other (in which consciousness is also present) perceives the first two, so that now there are three selves and three others; and the process continues indefinitely. And so multiplicity arises.

So far nothing I have said accounts for the single most crucial thing in the universe: change. Even granted that a self should perceive an other, what keeps the two from being frozen in an eternal embrace, as Shiva and Parvati are at the beginning of the story of the dice game?

The answer, in the language of the myth, is Narada, the malign yogi. Narada symbolizes separation. But it is not just a matter of separation. As we've already seen, one of the main characteristics of *purusha* is its capacity to identify with its experience. This implies the corresponding capacity to separate itself from experience, as happens when Narada introduces his version of strip

Parcheesi. It is this dynamic — *purusha*'s capacity to both identify with and detach itself from *prakriti* — that gives rise to the world in all its forms. We might even say that this is the only real variable in the universe; all others are dependent on it.

Up to this point I've discussed this interplay mostly in terms of human consciousness. Naturally: this book is written by a human for other humans, and our own minds and experiences are of central importance to us. But what if we were to view this interplay in somewhat broader terms, say, as it might operate in supposedly inanimate matter?

To begin with, we have to recognize that change is not, or not entirely, random. It proceeds along a path that is predictable and consistent, at least to a degree. We might say that, in a given circumstance, *purusha* identifies with and separates from *prakriti* within a narrow frame and with a certain rhythm: it goes in and out in a reasonably consistent pattern. If this is the case, it might explain the principle we call vibration, which is, of course, known not only to science but to esoteric thought as well. ("Nothing rests; everything moves; everything vibrates," according to *The Kybalion*, an esoteric text from the early twentieth century.)[6] If this vibration is sufficiently rapid, it might appear to an observer as a solid, just as a fan spinning very fast looks like a solid plate. Hence our notion of matter as a set of particles.

If this is the case, the vibrations of *purusha* and *prakriti* will have to extend not only beyond the range of our scientific apparatus but also beyond the limits of the mind, even of a mind like Swedenborg's or Andreev's. Consequently everything we call real, and even everything we call unreal, is merely an infinitesimally small slice of a continuum so much larger that it's impossible for our limited cognition to grasp, just as an ant will never be able to comprehend the biology of its own nature.

It's possible for a scientific imagination to use these ideas for inspiration (much as Einstein is said to have kept a copy of Blavatsky's *Secret Doctrine* on his desk), but a scientific imagination is something I don't have. In any event, it's of very little value for anyone outside to tell science what to do or think. Science is not a doctrine or a dogma but a method — specifically a method that relies on empirical evidence to learn about physical reality. It will reach its own conclusions in its own time. It will only be constrained and impeded by dogmatists, whether they take the form of evangelists hawking a rehashed creationism or materialistic camp followers who want to turn Darwinism into the next new faith. Writing in the *New York Times* on the two-hundredth anniversary of Darwin's birth, Carl Safina, president of the Blue Ocean Institute, argues, "Our understanding of how life works since Darwin won't swim in the public pool of ideas until we kill the cult of Darwinism."[7]

In any case, the scientific enterprise seems to be converging on a single point. Anthropologists are investigating how many of our most cherished characteristics are simply those of highly developed apes; cognitive scientists are poking the brain to see how it constructs the homunculus of the self; and physicists are studying how and in what way the observer affects the phenomenon. Whatever these disciplines conclude about their particular subjects, in each case the enterprise is leading toward one central point: the nature of consciousness.

The most obvious case is psychology. The beginning of this discipline in its current form is often dated to 1900, with the publication of Freud's *The Interpretation of Dreams*. Strictly speaking, Freud's chief concern was not with consciousness but with its opposite: the unconscious drives and fears that truly motivate our actions and for which the ego has to make excuses as it can. Jung, building on Freud's insights, posited that these unconscious drives are universal and are revealed in myth and religious symbolism. Today comparatively few psychologists would describe themselves as pure Freudians or Jungians, but practically no one will deny that these unconscious forces operate at a deep level and often dictate behavior more urgently than do conscious choices.

Neither Freud nor Jung claimed, however, that these deeper reaches of the psyche were irrevocably unconscious, or that consciousness could not make progress in examining them; indeed, that was the whole point of their therapies. In one case, a female analysand was afraid of going outdoors. Her reason, she said, was her fear of falling down and having people see her lying in the street. Through analysis, she was able to see that she was actually guilty about her sexual adventures in the past and was afraid of repeating them; she was, both literally and metaphorically, afraid of becoming a "fallen woman."[8] Presumably the simple fact of this realization was enough to help her overcome her phobia or, at any rate, to take away some of its power over her. In any case, it's safe to say that a person who has this kind of insight into her behavior can never see it in quite the same light again.

Contemporary psychotherapy, the heir to Freud and Jung, is prone to fads and absurdities; it is also a slow and clumsy method, and even successful practitioners are not always able to articulate what they actually do to help their clients. Nonetheless, it has been of tremendous benefit to millions of people, and much of this benefit has to do with making the unconscious conscious.

Gurdjieff's practice of self-observation differs from psychotherapy, but some of the points he makes about self-observation apply here as well:

> By observing himself [a man] throws, as it were, a ray of
> light onto his inner processes which have hitherto worked in

complete darkness. And under the influence of this light the processes themselves begin to change. There are a great many chemical processes that can take place only in the absence of light. Exactly in the same way many psychic processes can take place only in the dark. Even a feeble light of consciousness is enough to change completely the character of a process, while it makes many of them altogether impossible.[9]

Parallel to this psychology of introspection is the trend toward probing into the physical mechanisms of consciousness. This includes not only neurobiology and neurochemistry but also genetic research. In the *New York Times Magazine*, Harvard psychology professor Steven Pinker explains why he decided to have his personal genetic sequence mapped out and published on the Internet. Part of it was a quest for self-knowledge. "The plunging cost of genome sequencing," he writes, "will soon give people an unprecedented opportunity to contemplate their own biological and even psychological makeups." The actual value of these genetic maps for self-awareness is moot: Pinker admits that he found himself using his own psychological insights to interpret the genetic readouts rather than the other way around.[10]

Despite this caveat, even the clinical and soulless procedures of genetic mapping have a goal that is not far from that of the introspective approaches: they are meant to increase our understanding of how consciousness manifests in us. The point is not that scientists or philosophers or humanity as a whole will ever totally agree about how the mind operates, but simply that it is becoming a large-scale project of civilization to explore this question.

Then there is computer science. According to the contemporary philosopher John R. Searle, theorists tend to describe the mind in terms of the dominant technology of their time: Freud portrayed it as a kind of hydraulic or electromagnetic system, with the drives of the id harnessed by the superego in service to the ego. Others have seen it as a telegraph or a switchboard. Today one of the most fascinating forms of technology is computers, so there has been no end of philosophers who have described the mind merely as a hypersophisticated computer.[11] In his book *Rapture for the Geeks*, Richard Dooling offers some fairly standard reflections in the wake of his visit to Firefly, a supercomputer housed in Omaha:

> Even if Firefly can't yet think for itself, what about ten or twenty Firefly supercomputers networked together? What about a billion computers...harnessed by a company like Google? Would those be capable of mimicking human intelligence, assuming someone, or some supercomputer, came along and wrote the proper software?
>
> Other questions soon follow: If a supercomputer ever does "think" the way human brains do, how will we know it? Will it be "conscious" in the same way we are? Do these questions make sense given the trouble we've had over the centuries describing human or animal consciousness?[12]

Some have no doubts about the answer. Douglas R. Hofstadter, author of *Gödel, Escher, Bach*, insists, "Minds exist in brains and may come to exist in programmed machines. If and when such machines come about, their causal powers will derive not from the substances they are made of, but from their design and the programs that run in them. And the way we will know they have those causal powers is by talking to them and listening carefully to what they have to say."[13] This passage comes from Hofstadter's reply to Searle's essay "Minds, Brains, and Programs," which argued the opposite: that a computer program, no matter how sophisticated, can't replicate the intentionality of brain-based cognition, even if it appears to do so. Philosophers like Hofstadter, who argue for "strong AI" — the idea that a computer can be developed with cognition like our own — do so on the grounds of verification. If a computer responds in such a way that it can't be distinguished from a human, it can be said to be conscious. (This, incidentally, is called the Turing test, after the British computer pioneer Alan Turing, who came up with the idea.)

Of course this supposed verification is purely speculative: no computer has been developed with anything close to this capacity. Even if a computer were to pass the Turing test, other philosophers have doubts about what this would really prove. Searle mentions a curious computer program called ELIZA. First written in 1966 by Joseph Weizenbaum, it parodies the responses of a therapist. Today it's easily accessible on the Internet,[14] and for some reason Macintosh OSX comes bundled with a bug-ridden version of it. Here's a sample conversation with ELIZA:

> ELIZA: Hello. How can I help you?
> RS: I'm feeling lonely.
> ELIZA: Does it please you to believe i [*sic*] am feeling lonely?
> RS: No, not really.
> ELIZA: You are being a bit negative.
> RS: I'm just trying to find out what you mean.
> ELIZA: Does it please you to believe i am just trying to find out what i mean?
> RS: No, not really.
> ELIZA: You are being a bit negative.

As you can see, ELIZA is a crude piece of software. Despite this, and despite the fact that it was written as a joke, large numbers of people (somewhat alarmingly) have found it helpful. If ELIZA's bland redundancies seem simpleminded, many human therapists don't do much better. The website I visited to create the sample dialogue displays the slogan "ELIZA — a friend you could never have before."

The point is that you could find ELIZA helpful, and you might even come to think of it as a person, but you would be hard-pressed to argue that this program (or even a much improved version of it) could possess anything like human consciousness. Searle seems to be right when he says that our biological makeup bestows an intentionality on us that a machine could never replicate. Moreover, advocates of "strong AI" frequently talk as if the human mind does nothing but compute. But a large quantity of the mind has to do with irrational elements — dreams, fantasies, mystical experiences — that science does not fully understand and is not even close to being able to simulate. And what about that most human characteristic of all — conflict? The ancient Roman poet Catullus writes, "I hate and love. 'Why do you do this?' you may ask. / I don't know, but I feel it happen and am in anguish."[15] This is not the kind of response you can easily replicate with strings of ones and zeros, but it may be far more integral to human consciousness than is the ability to find the best move on a chessboard.

All this is to say that theorists who warn of an imminent "technological singularity" — in which we will have to confront machines that are smarter than we are — are probably about as deluded as prophets of most stripes. We already have computers that are better than we are at tallying stock market data and playing chess. But it would be extremely difficult to ascribe consciousness of any human sort to these machines, much less argue that they are about to become our masters.

All this said, the problem of artificial intelligence is not quite as acute for the theory presented in this book as it is for most types of philosophy, for the simple reason that I have not posited a radical, unbridgeable barrier between animate and supposedly inanimate consciousness. While a computer has a very primitive capacity to relate self and other, it does possess consciousness *of a kind*. But then, as we've seen, so do hydrogen atoms and water molecules. I'm not arguing for a kind of ghost in the machine here. Rather I'm saying that the mere capacity to recognize and respond is a form of consciousness, no matter how rudimentary and automatic compared to our own. We utilize it in every tool we make. It's such a fundamental part of the universe that we rarely notice it.

Such are the scientific implications of the ideas in this book, at least in extremely broad terms. In any event, they go some way toward suggesting how consciousness, rather than being an anomaly or an epiphenomenon, is integral to the structure of the universe — at least of any universe that is knowable to us.

These reflections all suggest that the aims of both science and religion are finding a point of convergence: the centrality of consciousness. For religion, particularly Christianity, the task is to abandon the conceptual barricades that separate the "I" of the inner self from the "I" of God. For science, the task is to break down its conceptual barrier between human consciousness and all other kinds. After all, it's difficult to conceive of anything that exists without a basis in the polarity of self and other. And this, as we've seen, implies consciousness in some form.

Indeed consciousness may become the focal point of civilization in the third millennium. Since the eighteenth century, Western civilization has been living in a kind of spiritual interregnum. Christianity, which a few centuries ago dominated all intellectual life in the West, has waned to the point where it is only one of a number of worldviews that vie for allegiance. The same is true for the other great religions in their own contexts — Buddhism, Hinduism, Islam, and so on. What has largely replaced the religious vision is a civilization of utility, in which political, economic, and technological concerns have been the chief forces holding society together. While humankind has made tremendous gains in these areas, ultimately these gains will not be enough to give purpose and meaning to life. As Nietzsche saw, man needs to overcome himself, and this requires him to reach beyond the narrow limits of his own self-concepts. A few individuals throughout the ages have done this, but it is a goal that civilization as a whole has hardly sought at all. Of previous civilizations, some were focused on propitiating the gods through sacrifice; some (medieval Christendom, for example) were meant to serve as placeholders for the coming kingdom of God; and others, such as ancient Rome and imperial England, claimed that their ideal was to spread justice and order to the undomesticated sections of humanity. Hindu and Buddhist civilizations may have the aim of self-knowledge in the background, but this knowledge has been reserved for a few adepts. Today, however, civilization as a whole — and I mean the world civilization that is emerging, not the West or the developed world alone — is moving toward the aim of exploring consciousness, whether this manifests through psychological introspection, neurological research, or work with artificial intelligence.

My intent here is not to hoist any flags or lead any charges up hills. I'm not saying that civilization *should* have this aim — although it is a good one — but rather that it's already moving in this direction willy-nilly. If we need to justify it pragmatically, delving into the nature of consciousness may help us avoid any number of mistakes both in our personal lives and in society at large. Understanding the nature of love could prevent much of the pain that afflicts the human heart whenever it opens itself to another. Knowing how we behave in terms of labor and interchange can help us plan our economies, personal and national, more smoothly and effectively — and so on.

In the end, however, the quest to know ourselves outstrips any pragmatic applications. To all appearances, we are the only creatures who seek knowledge for its own sake, not just because it could help us find richer sources of food or mate with better specimens. The serpent in Genesis told the primordial couple that if they ate the fruit of knowledge, they would be as gods, knowing good and evil. The serpent did not lie. He did not, it's true, spell out all the consequences of this act — for to know good and evil is to know the world as we have it, with its interwoven joys and pains.

Even so, if we were collectively given the choice, we might well do the same thing all over again. Hence the ancient Gnostics could see the serpent as a figure not of evil but of liberation. Odysseus too chose to know what the Sirens' song was like even though it caused him immeasurable anguish to hear it. I've often thought that the purpose of humanity is to collectively experience the full range of possibilities available on this earth. Certainly it seems that, if you can think of anything that is physically possible, however sublime or however foul, there is someone somewhere who has tried to do it. When the human race finally departs from this planet, it may be that we will do so having collectively exhausted the possibilities of knowledge and experience that it has to offer. Ultimately, as the sages remind us, the individual *purusha* will pour itself out into the ocean of limitless mind.

Does all of this imply progress or evolution? There is the temptation, when spreading out grand perspectives, to invoke these concepts, but I don't know that they are anything more than imaginary constructs that we use to motivate ourselves. Sometimes we seem to be progressing, sometimes not; sometimes our very progress seems to make things worse. And while evolution seems to have some direction — toward greater complexity if nothing else — the Darwinian theory may be right in saying that there is no purpose in it, that it is merely the result of adventitious adaptations by quintillions of organisms across the ages. Or as the Samkhya might say, the *gunas* interact endlessly without beginning or end. Regardless of whether we progress or whether the cycle perpetuates itself endlessly, in the midst of it all remains consciousness, awake or asleep, enlightened or deluded, everywhere cramped and constrained yet also eternally infinite and unstained, just as Shiva perpetually loses the dice game while actually losing nothing.

NOTES

CHAPTER 1. *The Light That Governs the Universe*

1. The letter is to be found in Dietrich Bonhoeffer, *Letters and Papers from Prison*, ed. Eberhard Bethge, trans. Reginald Fuller et al., rev. ed. (New York: Touchstone, 1997), 324–29.

2. W. W. Rouse Ball, *A Short Account of the History of Mathematics*, 4th ed. (1908); Trinity College Dublin School of Mathematics, www.maths.tcd.ie/pub/HistMath/People/Laplace/RouseBall/RB _Laplace.html, accessed on Oct. 16, 2007.

3. Immanuel Kant, *Critique of Practical Reason*, quoted in "The Cambridge Companion to Kant and Modern Philosophy," http://cco.cambridge.org/extract?id=ccol052182303X _CCOL052182303XA001, accessed on Oct. 17, 2007.

4. "Patience, Fairness, and the Human Condition," *The Economist*, Oct. 6, 2007, 93–94.

5. Ibid.

6. Bonhoeffer, 360.

7. Tertullian, *On the Flesh of Christ*, §5. This statement is often quoted as "Credo quia absurdum": "I believe because it is absurd." On this point see H. Richard Niebuhr, *Christ and Culture* (San Francisco: Harper & Row, 1951), 77; also see ch. 7 below.

8. Daniel Dennett, *Darwin's Dangerous Idea* (New York: Simon & Schuster, 1995), 184–85. Emphasis added.

9. Christof Koch and Susan Greenfield, "How Does Consciousness Happen?" *Scientific American*, Oct. 2007, 76. Emphasis here and in other quotations is in the original unless otherwise noted.

10. Dennett, *Darwin's Dangerous Idea*, 63.

11. Richard Dawkins, *The Selfish Gene* (New York: Oxford University Press, 1976), 210–11.

12. Mary Midgley, *Evolution as a Religion*, rev. ed. (London: Routledge, 2002), 144–45.

13. BBC Manchester home page, www.bbc.co.uk/manchester/content/ articles/2008/06/04/040608_peppered_moth_feature.shtml, accessed on March 13, 2009.

14. Richard Milton, *Shattering the Myths of Darwinism*, 2nd ed. (Rochester, Vt.: Park Street Press, 1997), 130–31.

15. Midgley, 94.

16. John Shelby Spong, *Jesus for the Non-Religious* (San Francisco: HarperSanFrancisco, 2007), 275.

17. John Shelby Spong, *A New Christianity for a New World: Why Traditional Faith Is Dying and How a New Faith Is Being Born* (San Francisco: HarperSanFrancisco, 2002), 54.

18. Eric Pace, "A. J. Ayer Dead in Britain at 78; Dean of Logical Positivism," *New York Times*, June 28, 1989; http://query.nytimes.com/ gst/fullpage.html?res=950DEEDB1730F93AA15755C0A96F948260 &sec=&spon=&pagewanted=2, accessed on Oct. 25, 2007.

19. Hippocrates, *On the Sacred Disease*, trans. Francis Adams; Spirituality and the Brain website, www.shaktitechnology.com/hippocrat.htm, accessed on Oct. 27, 2007.

20. See, for example, Daniel C. Dennett, review of *Problem of Consciousness*, by Colin McGinn, *Times Literary Supplement*, May 10, 1991; Tufts University website, http://ase.tufts.edu/cogstud/papers/ mcginn.htm, accessed on Feb. 12, 2008.

21. John Woodroffe, *The Serpent Power*, 7th ed. (Madras: Ganesh, 1964), 30. *Cit* is also transliterated as *chit* or *chitta*.

22. George Parsons Lathrop, "Talks with Edison," *Harper's New Monthly Magazine*, Feb. 1890, 435.

23. Richard Smoley, "Toxic Prayer: An Interview with Larry Dossey," *Gnosis* 47 (spring 1998): 31.

24. Lawrence LeShan, *A New Science of the Paranormal: The Promise of Psychical Research* (Wheaton, Ill.: Quest, 2009), 15.

CHAPTER 2. *The Game of Consciousness*

1. For this myth, I rely on Don Handelman and David Shulman, *God Inside Out: Siva's Game of Dice* (New York: Oxford University Press, 1997), 17–20.

2. Rig Veda 10.129.2, trans. David Shulman; in Handelman and Shulman, *God Inside Out*, 46. Bracketed insertion is Shulman's.

3. John Locke, *An Essay Concerning Human Understanding*, ed. Peter H. Nidditch (Oxford: Clarendon Press, 1975), 4.3, §6.

4. Ibid., 4.10.

5. Brihadaranyaka Upanishad, 3.4.2; *Thirteen Principal Upanishads*, rev. ed., trans. R. E. Hume (London: Oxford University Press, 1931), 112.

6. "Who," in *Maha Yoga, or the Upanishadic Lore in the Light of the Teachings of Sri Ramana Maharshi*, 4th ed. (Tiruvannamalai, India: Sri Niranjananda Swamy, Sri Ramanasramam, 1950), 127–28.

7. Heraclitus, fragment 2; in G. S. Kirk and J. E. Raven, *The Presocratic Philosophers* (Cambridge: Cambridge University Press, 1957), 188. My translation.

8. Biblical quotations in this book are taken from the Authorized King James Version.

9. Arthur Schopenhauer, *The World as Will and Representation*, trans. E. F. J. Payne (New York: Dover, 1966), 2:5.

10. Ibid., 1:30.

11. Ibid., 1:129–30.

12. George Berkeley, *A Treatise Concerning the Principles of Human Knowledge*, §§1, 3; University of Oregon website, www.uoregon.edu/~rbear/berkeley.html#treat, accessed on Feb. 17, 2008.

13. George Berkeley, *Third Dialogue between Hylas and Philonous*, in Charles William Eliot, ed., *The Harvard Classics*, vol. 37: *English Philosophers of the Seventeenth and Eighteenth Centuries: Locke, Berkeley, Hume* (New York: P. P. Collier, 1910), 267.

14. Plato, *Republic*, trans. Robin Waterfield (Oxford: Oxford University Press, 1993), 479c–d.
15. Andrija Puharich, *Beyond Telepathy* (London: Souvenir, 1974), 33–34.
16. Daniel Pinchbeck, "Absorbing Orbs," Reality Sandwich website, www.realitysandwich.com/absorbing_orbs, accessed on Sept. 23, 2008.
17. Charles Dickens, *Hard Times*, ch. 2.
18. Brihadaranyaka Upanishad, 1.3.28. *Sat* and *asat* literally mean "being" and "nonbeing," so the thrust of the prayer is very much like Plato's argument in *The Republic*.
19. Woodroffe, *The Serpent Power*, 291–92.

CHAPTER 3. *Two against One*

1. Richard Cavendish, *The Black Arts* (New York: Putnam, 1967), 75–76.
2. For a brief survey of the issues surrounding dualism in the philosophy of mind, see Kwame Anthony Appiah, *Thinking It Through: An Introduction to Contemporary Philosophy* (New York: Oxford University Press, 2003), 5–12.
3. For more on these movements, see my book *Forbidden Faith: The Secret History of Gnosticism* (San Francisco: HarperSanFrancisco, 2006), chs. 3 and 4.
4. P. D. Ouspensky, *The Psychology of Man's Possible Evolution* (New York: Knopf, 1972), 109.
5. Stephen Larsen, *The Fundamentalist Mind: How Polarized Thinking Imperils Us All* (Wheaton, Ill.: Quest, 2007), 42.
6. Soc.religion.christian newsgroup, http://geneva.rutgers.edu/src/index.html, accessed on March 3, 2008.
7. Center for Non-Dualism, www.centerfornondualism.org/, accessed on March 3, 2008.
8. Matthew Fox, *The Coming of the Cosmic Christ* (San Francisco: Harper & Row, 1988), 233, 134–35.
9. Heinrich Zimmer, *Philosophies of India*, ed. Joseph Campbell (London: Routledge & Kegan Paul, 1952), 280. The quotation is from the Bhagavad Gita, 5.4–5. Zimmer's transliterations of Sanskrit terms, like most scholarly versions, include diacritical marks that I have omitted here. Hence the differences in spelling between Sanskrit

terms in direct quotes and in my own usage (*sankhya* vs. *samkhya*, for example). My transliterations are English phonetic equivalents of the Sanskrit that are close enough for the purposes of the general reader. Parenthetical insertions here and in other quotations are in the original.

10. H. P. Blavatsky, *The Secret Doctrine*, 3rd Point Loma ed. (Point Loma, Calif.: Aryan Theosophical Press, 1925), 2:571.

11. Gerald J. Larson, *Classical Samkhya*, rev. ed. (Delhi: Motilal Banarsidass, 1979), 96; R. C. Zaehner, ed. and trans., *The Bhagavad-Gita* (New York: Oxford University Press, 1969), 7.

12. Larson, *Classical Samkhya*, 4.

13. K. B. Ramakrishna Rao, *Theism of Pre-Classical Samkhya* (Prasangara, India: University of Mysore, 1966), 3.

14. Larson, *Classical Samkhya*, 278.

15. For the dates of Sri Anirvan's life, see Lizelle Reymond, *To Live Within* (Portland, Ore.: Rudra Press, 1995), xviii.

16. Ishvarakrishna, *Samkhyakarika*, 19, 20; in Larson, *Classical Samkhya*, 262.

17. Larson, *Classical Samkhya*, 13.

18. Ibid., 10–11.

19. Ibid., 93.

20. *Samkhyakarika*, 65–66; in Larson, *Classical Samkhya*, 275. Parenthetical insertions are the translator's.

21. Larson, *Classical Samkhya*, 135.

22. Ibid., 134–35.

23. *Samkhyakarika*, 18; in Larson, *Classical Samkhya*, 261.

24. Zimmer, *Philosophies of India*, 285.

25. *The Rig Veda*, ed. and trans. Wendy Doniger O'Flaherty (London: Penguin, 1981), 10.90; pp. 30–31.

26. See P. N. Srinivasachari, *The Philosophy of Visistadvaita* (Adyar, India: Adyar Library and Research Centre, 1943), for a discussion of some of these.

27. Shvestashvarata Upanishad, 3.13.

28. Hans Torwesten, *Vedanta: Heart of Hinduism* (New York: Grove Weidenfield, 1991), 125.

29. Shankara, *Shankara's Crest-Jewel of Discrimination*, trans. Swami Prabhavananda and Christopher Isherwood (Hollywood: Vedanta Press, 1947), 98.

30. Sankaracharya [*sic*], *Dakshinamurti Stotra*, trans. Alladi Mahadeva Shastry, 3rd ed. (Madras: Samata, 1978), §8. Depending on the transliteration of the Sanskrit, the philosopher's name is variously spelled as "Sankaracharya" and "Shankaracharya." Often it is abbreviated to "Shankara" or "Sankara." He is generally thought to have lived in the late eighth and early ninth centuries. But possible dates range from AD 650 to 800. See Natalia Isayeva, *Shankara and Indian Philosophy* (Albany: State University of New York Press, 1993), 75–87.

31. Shankara, *Shankara's Crest-Jewel of Discrimination*, 49.

32. Quoted in Kshitish Chandra Chakravarti, *Vision of Reality* (Calcutta: Firma K. L. Mukhopadhyay, 1969), 180.

33. Shankara, introduction to *Shankara's Crest-Jewel of Discrimination*, 18.

34. Shankara, *Shankara's Crest-Jewel of Discrimination*, 55.

35. Shankara, introduction to *Shankara's Crest-Jewel of Discrimination*, 15.

36. Shankara, *Shankara's Crest-Jewel of Discrimination*, 134, 43.

37. Reymond, *To Live Within*, 63–64.

38. On this point, see Krishna Prem, *The Yoga of the Bhagavat Gita* (Shaftesbury, Dorset, U.K.: Element, 1988), 146.

39. Quoted in Marcia Binder Schmidt, *The Dzogchen Primer: Embracing the Spiritual Path according to the Great Perfection* (Boston: Shambhala, 2002), 209. Emphasis added.

CHAPTER 4. *Constant Conjunction*

1. Plato, *Timaeus*, 28a. For a good summary of the various views of causation in Western philosophy, see Menno Hulswit, "A Brief History of 'Causation,'" University of Toronto Libraries website, www.library.utoronto.ca/see/SEED/Vol4-3/Hulswit.htm, accessed on June 23, 2008.

2. Henri Frankfort et al., *Before Philosophy* (Harmondsworth, Middlesex, U.K.: Pelican, 1949), 26.

3. Aristotle, *The Physics*, ed. and trans. Philip H. Wicksteed and Francis M. Cornford (Cambridge, Mass.: Loeb Classical Library, 1934), 8.6, 258b.

4. Bertrand Russell, "On the Notion of Cause," 1; quoted on Stanford Encyclopedia of Philosophy website, http://plato.stanford.edu/entries/causation-process/, accessed on July 16, 2008.

5. Aristotle, *Physics*, 2.3, 194b23–195a3; *Metaphysics*, 7.7, 1032a11–1032b23.

6. Some philosophers suggest *explanation* or other terms. See Anthony Kenny, *A New History of Western Philosophy*, vol. 1: *Ancient Philosophy* (Oxford: Clarendon, 2004), 190.

7. Hulswit, "A Brief History of 'Causation.'"

8. David Hume, *A Treatise of Human Nature*, ed. David Fate Norton and Mary Norton (Oxford: Oxford University Press, 2000), 1.3.2.

9. Ibid., 1.3.6.

10. David Hume, *Enquiries Concerning the Human Understanding and Concerning the Principles of Morals*, ed. L. A. Selby-Bigge, 2nd ed. (Oxford: Clarendon Press, 1902), 7.2.

11. Augustine, *Confessions*, trans. R. S. Pine-Coffin (New York: Dorset, 1986), 11.14.

12. Maurice Nicoll, *Living Time and the Integration of the Life* (London: Vincent Stuart, 1952), 142.

13. Lawrence LeShan, *A New Science of the Paranormal: The Promise of Psychical Research* (Wheaton, Ill.: Quest, 2009), 124.

14. Bertrand Russell, *The Problems of Philosophy* (1912; reprint, New York: Barnes & Noble, 2004), 42.

15. Immanuel Kant, *Prolegomena to Any Future Metaphysics*, trans. Paul Carus (Indianapolis: Bobbs, Merrill, 1950), 8. For a list of the categories, see Immanuel Kant, *Critique of Pure Reason*, trans. J. M. D. Meiklejohn (New York: Wiley, n.d.), 111–12.

16. Schopenhauer, *The World as Will and Representation*, 1:446.

17. Kant, *Critique of Pure Reason*, 197 ff.

18. Roger Penrose, *The Emperor's New Mind* (Oxford: Oxford University Press, 1989), 302.

19. The definition was popularized by Thomas Aquinas. Thomas attributed it to a tenth-century Jewish philosopher named Isaac Israëli, but scholars have not been able to find it in Israëli's works. See History

and Theory of Ontology website, www.formalontology.it/
veritas.htm, accessed on Jan. 26, 2009.

20. Quoted in Jacques Derrida, *Of Grammatology*, trans. Gayatri
Chakravorty Spivak (Baltimore: Johns Hopkins University Press,
1976), 49.

21. Ibid., 22–23.

22. Hume, *Treatise of Human Nature*, 1.4.7.

23. Plato, *Republic*, trans. Robin Waterfield (Oxford: Oxford University
Press, 1993), 514b–c.

24. Ibid., 516c–d.

25. *The Rig Veda*, ed. and trans. Wendy Doniger O'Flaherty (London:
Penguin, 1981), 10.129.

26. *Samkhyakarika*, 22; in Larson, *Classical Samkhya*, 194.

27. *Samkhyakarika*, 31; in Larson, *Classical Samkhya*, 207.

28. K. C. Bhattacharya, in *Samkhya: A Dualist Tradition in Indian Philos-
ophy*, ed. Gerald J. Larson and Ram Shankar Bhattacharya, vol. 4 of
Encyclopedia of Indian Philosophies (Princeton: Princeton University
Press, 1987), 70.

29. *Sankhyakarika*, 1; in Larson, *Classical Samkhya*, 257.

30. Larson and Bhattacharya, 387.

31. See ibid., 68–72.

CHAPTER 5. *Patterns in Her Garment*

1. Khenchen Palden Sherab and Khenpo Tsewang Dongyal, *Opening to
Our Primordial Nature*, 2nd ed. (Ithaca, N.Y.: Snow Lion, 2006), 74.

2. Namkhai Norbu, *Dzogchen: The Self-Perfected State*, trans. John
Shane (Ithaca, N.Y.: Snow Lion, 1996), 81.

3. Clark Wissler, *Red Man Reservations* (New York: Collier-Macmillan,
1972), 203.

4. In Larson and Bhattacharya, 81.

5. Brihadaranyaka Upanishad, 3.27.

6. Heraclitus, fragment 21 DK; in M. Marcovich, ed. and trans.,
Heraclitus (Merida, Venezuela: Los Andes University Press, 1967),
247. My translation.

7. C. Binz, quoted in Sigmund Freud, *The Interpretation of Dreams*, trans. Joyce Crick (Oxford: Oxford University Press, 1999), 49.

8. Lev Nikolayevich Tolstoy, *Anna Karenina*, trans. Margaret Wettlin (Moscow: Progress, 1978), 1:30.

9. See, for example, NASA's website, http://universe.nasa.gov/press/2003/030521b.html, accessed on Oct. 13, 2008.

10. For a valuable account of the relation of the Samkhya to Gurdjieff's teachings, see Lizelle Reymond, *To Live Within* (Portland, Ore.: Rudra Press, 1995).

11. Alla Andreeva, foreword to *The Rose of the World*, by Daniel Andreev, trans. Jordan Roberts (Hudson, N.Y.: Lindisfarne, 1996), xiv.

12. Andreev, *The Rose of the World*, 230, 235.

13. Guy Lyon Playfair, "Has CSICOP (Committee for the Scientific Investigation of the Claims of the Paranormal) Lost the 30 Years' War?," Media Watch website; www.skepticalinvestigations.org/observer/30yearswar_2.htm, accessed Dec. 12, 2008.

14. C. G. Jung, *Synchronicity: An Acausal Connecting Principle*, trans. R. F. C. Hull (Princeton: Princeton/Bollingen, 1973), 22.

15. Ibid., 20, 24.

16. Ibid., 100.

17. Blavatsky, *The Secret Doctrine*, 1:44.

18. *The Rig Veda*, ed. and trans. Wendy Doniger O'Flaherty (London: Penguin, 1981), 10.25.7.

CHAPTER 6. *A Just Universe?*

1. Denise Gellene, "U.S. Suicide Rate Is Up," *Los Angeles Times*, Oct. 21, 2008; www.latimes.com/news/science/la-sci-suicide21-2008oct21,0,838216.story, accessed on Dec. 17, 2008.

2. Reinhold Niebuhr, *The Nature and Destiny of Man* (Louisville, Ky.: Westminster/John Knox, 1964), 2:56.

3. Longchenpa, *Kindly Bent to Ease Us*, trans. Herbert V. Guenther (Berkeley, Calif.: Dharma), 1:30.

4. In G. W. Butterworth, ed. and trans., *Origen: On First Principles* (New York: Harper & Row, 1966), 126.

5. Origen, *Commentary on Matthew*, 13:1; quoted on the Catholic Answers website, www.catholic.com/library/Reincarnation.asp, accessed on Dec. 22, 2008. This page quotes a valuable selection of excerpts from the church fathers on reincarnation.

6. *St. Anthony Messenger* website, www.americancatholic.org/ messenger/Mar2000/Wiseman.asp, accessed on Dec. 22, 2008.

7. See Harris Interactive website, www.harrisinteractive.com/harris _poll/index.asp?PID=838, accessed on Dec. 29, 2008.

8. Emanuel Swedenborg, *Heaven and Hell*, trans. George F. Dole, rev. ed. (West Chester, Pa.: Swedenborg Foundation, 2000), §479 (p. 364); also §58 (pp. 115–16).

9. Pandit Rajmani Tigunait, *Seven Systems of Indian Philosophy* (Honesdale, Pa.: Himalayan Institute Press, 1983), 24.

10. Bhagavad Gita, 4:19–20; in R. C. Zaehner, ed. and trans., *The Bhagavad-Gita* (New York: Oxford University Press, 1969), 59. Bracketed insertions are Zaehner's.

11. Dalai Lama, *The Meaning of Life: Buddhist Perspectives on Cause and Effect*, trans. Jeffrey Hopkins (Somerville, Mass.: Wisdom, 1992), 45.

12. D. T. Suzuki, *The Zen Doctrine of No-Mind*, ed. Christmas Humphreys, 2nd ed. (London: Rider, 1969), 36.

13. Brihadaranyaka Upanishad, ch. 6; in W. B. Yeats and Shree Purohit Swami, *The Ten Principal Upanishads* (New York: Macmillan, 1937), 143.

14. René Guénon, *Introduction to the Study of the Hindu Doctrines*, trans. Marco Pallis (New Delhi: Munshiram Manoharlal, 1993), 262.

CHAPTER 7. *Beyond the Copper Mountain*

1. Leslie D. Weatherhead, *The Christian Agnostic* (London: Stodder & Houghton, 1965), 28.

2. Quoted in Louis Dupré, *Kierkegaard as Theologian: The Dialectic of Christian Existence* (New York: Sheed & Ward, 1963), 113, 122.

3. Søren Kierkegaard, *Fear and Trembling*, ed. C. Stephen Evans and Sylvia Walsh (Cambridge: Cambridge University Press, 2006), 29, 31.

4. Cf. Dupré, 132–33.

5. Quoted in ibid., 123.

6. Kierkegaard, *Philosophical Fragments,* ch. 4; quoted in Dupré, *Kierkegaard as Theologian,* 203.

7. William James, "The Will to Believe," James Madison University website, http://falcon.jmu.edu/~omearam/ph101willtobelieve.html, accessed on May 15, 2008.

8. Paul Tillich, *Dynamics of Faith* (New York: Harper & Row, 1957).

9. Schopenhauer, *The World as Will and Representation,* 1:368.

10. Phillip Gowins, *The Sovereign Soul: Sufism, a Path for Today* (Boca Raton, Fla.: New Paradigm, 2006), 8–13.

11. Carl A. Anderson, *A Civilization of Love: What Every Catholic Can Do to Change the World* (San Francisco: HarperSanFrancisco, 2008), 123–24.

12. Cf. James, "The Will to Believe," 13.

13. Steven T. Katz, "Language, Epistemology, and Mysticism," in Katz, ed., *Mysticism and Philosophical Analysis* (New York: Oxford University Press, 1978), 33, 66.

14. William James, *The Varieties of Religious Experience* (New York: Longmans, Green, 1902), 380.

15. Xenophanes, fragment 15; in G. S. Kirk and J. E. Raven, *The Presocratic Philosophers* (Cambridge: Cambridge University Press, 1957), 169.

16. Xenophanes, fragment B32; in Kirk and Raven, *Presocratic Philosophers,* 173.

17. "Fake Medicinal 'Green Honey' Sold in the Philippines," *Apitherapy News,* March 28, 2008, http://apitherapy.blogspot.com/2008/03/fake-medicinal-honey-sold-in.html, accessed on June 14, 2008.

18. See Eleanor Irwin, *Colour Terms in Greek Poetry* (Toronto: Hakkert, 1974), for an extensive discussion of this point; also Rebecca Bird, "Language and Perception of Color among the Ancient Greeks," Cooper Union website, www.cooper.edu/classes/art/hta321/99spring/Rebecca.html, accessed on June 14, 2008.

19. Quoted in Arthur Osborne, ed., *The Teachings of Bhagavan Sri Ramana Maharshi in His Own Words* (London: Rider, 1962), 48.

20. Nisargadatta Maharaj, *The Experience of Nothingness,* ed. Robert Powell (San Diego: Blue Dove, 1996), 35.

21. The interchange appears in Osborne, 47–48.
22. Quoted on Fordham University website, www.fordham.edu/halsall/source/all-hallaj-quotations.html, accessed on June 17, 2008.
23. In Osborne, *Teachings of Bhagavan Sri Ramana Maharshi*, 43. The *Tiruvachakam* is a work of Tamil devotional literature of which Ramana Maharshi thought very highly.
24. For a similar view, see Plotinus, *The Enneads*, trans. Stephen MacKenna (Burdett, N.Y.: Larson, 1992), 3.8.8.

CHAPTER 8. *The Conscious Civilization*

1. For further discussion of these points, see my *Inner Christianity: A Guide to the Esoteric Tradition* (Boston: Shambhala, 2002), chs. 2 and 4.
2. Henry George Liddell and Robert Scott, *A Greek-English Lexicon*, ed. Henry Stuart Jones (Oxford: Oxford at the Clarendon Press, 1968), s.v. (*entós*).
3. *A Course in Miracles* (Tiburon, Calif.: Foundation for Inner Peace, 1975), 2:71.
4. Quoted in Jacques Lacan, *Écrits: A Selection*, trans. Alan Sheridan (New York: Norton, 1977), 128.
5. Martin Heidegger, *Early Greek Thinking*, trans. David Farrell Krell and Frank A. Capuzzi (New York: Harper & Row, 1975), 59–66.
6. Yogi Publication Society, "Three Initiates," *The Kybalion* (N.p.: Yogi Publication Society, 1908), 25.
7. Carl Safina, "Darwinism Must Die So That Evolution Can Live," *New York Times*, Feb. 9, 2009, www.nytimes.com/2009/02/10/science/10essa.html?pagewanted=1&_r=1, accessed on Feb. 15, 2009.
8. Philip Hill, *Lacan for Beginners* (New York: Writers & Readers, 1997), 10.
9. P. D. Ouspensky, *In Search of the Miraculous: Fragments of a Forgotten Teaching* (New York: Harcourt, Brace, 1949), 146.
10. Steven Pinker, "My Genome, My Self," *New York Times Magazine*, Jan. 7, 2009; www.nytimes.com/2009/01/11/magazine/11Genome-t.html?_r=1&ref=science, accessed on Jan. 12, 2009.

11. John R. Searle, *Minds, Brains, and Science* (Cambridge, Mass.: Harvard University Press, 1984), 44.

12. Richard Dooling, *Rapture for the Geeks: When AI Outsmarts IQ* (New York: Harmony, 2008), 2.

13. Douglas R. Hofstadter and Daniel Dennett, eds., *The Mind's I: Fantasies and Reflections on Self and Soul* (New York: Bantam, 1981), 382.

14. For one version, see the website Eliza: A Friend You Could Never Have Before, www-ai.ijs.si/eliza-cgi-bin/eliza_script, accessed on Jan. 13, 2009.

15. Catullus, 85; my translation.

BIBLIOGRAPHY

Anderson, Carl A. *A Civilization of Love: What Every Catholic Can Do to Change the World*. San Francisco: HarperSanFrancisco, 2008.

Andreev, Daniel. *The Rose of the World*. Translated by Jordan Roberts. Hudson, N.Y.: Lindisfarne, 1996.

Anselm. *Basic Writings*. Translated by S. N. Deane. 2nd ed. LaSalle, Ill.: Open Court, 1968.

Appiah, Kwame Anthony. *Thinking It Through: An Introduction to Contemporary Philosophy*. New York: Oxford University Press, 2003.

Aristotle. *The Basic Works of Aristotle*. Edited by Richard McKeon. New York: Random House, 1941.

———. *The Physics*. Edited and translated by Philip H. Wicksteed and Francis M. Cornford. 2 vols. Cambridge, Mass.: Loeb Classical Library, 1934.

Augustine. *Confessions*. Translated by R. S. Pine-Coffin. New York: Dorset, 1986.

Besant, Annie. *A Study in Consciousness*. 2nd ed. Adyar, India: Theosophical Publishing House, 1999.

Blavatsky, H. P. *The Secret Doctrine*. 3rd Point Loma ed. 2 vols. Point Loma, Calif.: Aryan Theosophical Press, 1925.

Boman, Thorleif. *Hebrew Thought Compared with Greek*. Translated by Jules L. Moreau. New York: Norton, 1970.

Bonhoeffer, Dietrich. *Letters and Papers from Prison*. Edited by Eberhard Bethge. Translated by Reginald Fuller et al. Rev. ed. New York: Touchstone, 1997.

Burkert, Walter. *Greek Religion*. Translated by John Raffan. Cambridge, Mass.: Harvard University Press, 1985.

Burnet, John, ed. *Platonis opera, tomus IV*. Oxford: Oxford University Press, 1901.

Butterworth, G. W., ed. and trans. *Origen: On First Principles*. New York: Harper & Row, 1966.

Catalina, Francis V. *A Study of the Self Concept of Sankhya-Yoga Philosophy*. Delhi: Munshiram Manarholal, 1968.

Cavendish, Richard. *The Black Arts*. New York: Putnam, 1967.

Chakravarti, Kshitish Chandra. *Vision of Reality*. Calcutta: Firma K. L. Mukhopadhyay, 1969.

A Course in Miracles. 3 vol. Tiburon, Calif.: Foundation for Inner Peace, 1975.

Dalai Lama. *The Meaning of Life: Buddhist Perspectives on Cause and Effect*. Translated by Jeffrey Hopkins. Somerville, Mass.: Wisdom, 1992.

Damiani, Anthony. *Astronoesis: Philosophy's Empirical Context, Astrology's Transcendental Ground*. Burdett, N.Y.: Larson, 2000.

Dasgupta, Surendranath. *A History of Indian Philosophy*. 5 vols. Cambridge: Cambridge University Press, 1922–55.

Dawkins, Richard. *The Selfish Gene*. New York: Oxford University Press, 1976.

Deikman, Arthur J. *The Observing Self: Mysticism and Psychotherapy*. Boston: Beacon, 1982.

Dennett, Daniel. *Breaking the Spell: Religion as a Natural Phenomenon*. New York: Penguin, 2006.

———. *Darwin's Dangerous Idea*. New York: Simon & Schuster, 1995.

———. *Sweet Dreams: Philosophical Objections to a Science of Consciousness*. Cambridge, Mass.: MIT Press, 2006.

Derrida, Jacques. *Of Grammatology*. Translated by Gayatri Chakravorty Spivak. Baltimore: Johns Hopkins University Press, 1976.

Deutsch, Eliot, and Rohit Dalvi, eds. *The Essential Vedanta: A New Source Book of Advaita Vedanta*. Bloomington, Ind.: World Wisdom, 2004.

Doniger, Wendy, ed. *Purana Perennis: Reciprocity and Transformation in Hindu and Jaina Texts*. Albany: State University of New York Press, 1993.

Dooling, Richard. *Rapture for the Geeks: When AI Outsmarts IQ*. New York: Harmony, 2008.

Dupré, Louis. *Kierkegaard as Theologian: The Dialectic of Christian Existence*. New York: Sheed & Ward, 1963.

Eliade, Mircea. *The Two and the One*. Translated by J. M. Cohen. Chicago: University of Chicago Press, 1965.

———. *Yoga: Immortality and Freedom*. New York: Pantheon/ Bollingen, 1958.

Eliot, Charles William, ed. *The Harvard Classics*. Vol. 37: *English Philosophers of the Seventeenth and Eighteenth Centuries: Locke, Berkeley, Hume*. New York: P. P. Collier, 1910.

The Encyclopedia of Philosophy. Edited by Paul Edwards. 8 vols. New York: Macmillan, 1967.

Fordyce, C. J., ed. *Catullus*. Oxford: Clarendon, 1961.

Fox, Matthew. *The Coming of the Cosmic Christ*. San Francisco: Harper & Row, 1988.

Frankfort, Henri, et al. *Before Philosophy*. Harmondsworth, Middlesex, U.K.: Pelican, 1949.

Freud, Sigmund. *The Interpretation of Dreams*. Translated by Joyce Crick. Oxford: Oxford University Press, 1999.

Goswami, Amit. *The Self-Aware Universe: How Consciousness Creates the Material World*. New York: Tarcher/Putnam, 1993.

Gowins, Phillip. *The Sovereign Soul: Sufism, a Path for Today*. Boca Raton, Fla.: New Paradigm, 2006.

The Greek New Testament. Edited by Kurt Aland et al. New York: United Bible Societies, 1966.

Griffiths, Bede. *Vedanta and Christian Faith*. Clearlake, Calif.: Dawn Horse, 1973.

Guénon, René. *Introduction to the Study of the Hindu Doctrines*. Translated by Marco Pallis. New Delhi: Munshiram Manoharlal, 1993.

————. *Man and His Becoming according to the Vedanta*. Translated by Richard C. Nicholson. New Delhi: Munshiram Manoharlal, 1981.

Handelman, Don, and David Shulman. *God Inside Out: Siva's Game of Dice*. New York: Oxford University Press, 1997.

Heidegger, Martin. *Early Greek Thinking*. Translated by David Farrell Krell and Frank A. Capuzzi. New York: Harper & Row, 1975.

Hill, Philip. *Lacan for Beginners*. New York: Writers & Readers, 1997.

Hofstadter, Douglas R., and Daniel Dennett, eds. *The Mind's I: Fantasies and Reflections on Self and Soul*. New York: Bantam, 1981.

Hume, David. *Enquiries Concerning the Human Understanding and Concerning the Principles of Morals*. Edited by L. A. Selby-Bigge. 2nd ed. Oxford: Clarendon, 1902.

————. *A Treatise of Human Nature*. Edited by David Fate Norton and Mary Norton. Oxford: Oxford University Press, 2000.

Irwin, Eleanor. *Colour Terms in Greek Poetry*. Toronto: Hakkert, 1974.

Isayeva, Natalia. *Shankara and Indian Philosophy*. Albany: State University of New York Press, 1993.

Iswara Krishna. *The Sankhya Karika, or Memorial Verses on the Indian Philosophy*. Translated by Henry Thomas Colebrook and Horace Hayman Wilson. London: Oxford University Press, 1837.

James, William. *The Varieties of Religious Experience*. New York: Longmans, Green, 1902.

Janet, Paul. *Final Causes*. Translated by William Affleck. New York: Charles Scribner's Sons, 1883.

Johnston, E. H. *Early Samkhya: An Essay on Its Historical Development according to the Texts*. London: Royal Asiatic Society, 1937.

Jung, C. G. *Synchronicity: An Acausal Connecting Principle*. Translated by R. F. C. Hull. Princeton: Princeton/Bollingen, 1973.

Kant, Immanuel. *Critique of Pure Reason*. Translated by J. M. D. Meiklejohn. New York: Wiley, n.d.

————. *Dreams of a Spirit-Seer and Other Writings*. Edited by Gregory R. Johnston. West Chester, Pa.: Swedenborg Foundation, 2002.

————. *Prolegomena to Any Future Metaphysics*. Translated by Paul Carus. Indianapolis: Bobbs, Merrill, 1950.

Katz, Steven T., ed. *Mysticism and Philosophical Analysis*. New York: Oxford University Press, 1978.

Kenny, Anthony. *A New History of Western Philosophy.* Vol. 1: *Ancient Philosophy.* Oxford: Clarendon, 2004.

Kern, Stephen. *A Cultural History of Causality: Science, Murder Novels, and Systems of Thought.* Princeton: Princeton University Press, 2004.

Kierkegaard, Søren. *Fear and Trembling.* Edited by C. Stephen Evans and Sylvia Walsh. Cambridge: Cambridge University Press, 2006.

Kirk, G. S., and J. E. Raven. *The Presocratic Philosophers.* Cambridge: Cambridge University Press, 1957.

Klostermaier, Klaus K. *A Survey of Hinduism.* 3rd ed. Albany: State University of New York Press, 2007.

Kunhan Raja, C. *Some Fundamental Problems in Indian Philosophy.* Delhi: Motilal Banarsidass, 1960.

Lacan, Jacques. *Écrits: A Selection.* Translated by Alan Sheridan. New York: Norton, 1977.

Langer, Ellen J. *Mindfulness.* Cambridge, Mass.: Perseus, 1989.

Larsen, Stephen. *The Fundamentalist Mind: How Polarized Thinking Imperils Us All.* Wheaton, Ill.: Quest, 2007.

Larson, Gerald J. *Classical Samkhya.* Rev. ed. Delhi: Motilal Banarsidass, 1979.

Larson, Gerald J., and Ram Shankar Bhattacharya, eds. *Samkhya: A Dualist Tradition in Indian Philosophy.* Vol. 4 of *Encyclopedia of Indian Philosophies.* Princeton: Princeton University Press, 1987.

LeShan, Lawrence. *A New Science of the Paranormal: The Promise of Psychical Research.* Wheaton, Ill.: Quest, 2009.

Liddell, Henry George, and Robert Scott. *A Greek-English Lexicon.* Edited by Henry Stuart Jones. Oxford: Clarendon, 1968.

Lindorf, David. *Pauli and Jung: The Meeting of Two Great Minds.* Wheaton, Ill.: Quest, 2004.

Locke, John. *An Essay Concerning Human Understanding.* Edited by Peter H. Nidditch. Oxford: Clarendon, 1975.

Longchenpa (Klong-chen rab-'byams-pa). *Kindly Bent to Ease Us.* Translated by Herbert V. Guenther. 3 vols. Berkeley, Calif.: Dharma, 1975–76.

Mackie, J. L. *The Cement of the Universe: A Study of Causation.* Oxford: Clarendon, 1974.

Mahacevan, T. M. P., ed. and trans. *The Hymns of Sankara*. Delhi: Motilal Banarsidass, 1980.

Manjusrimitra. *Primordial Experience: An Introduction to rDzogs-chen* [*sic*] *Meditation*. Translated by Namkhai Norbu and Kennard Lipman. Boston: Shambhala, 1983.

Marcovich, M., ed. and trans. *Heraclitus*. Merida, Venezuela: Los Andes University Press, 1967.

Merton, Thomas. *The Asian Journal of Thomas Merton*. Edited by Naomi Burton et al. New York: New Directions, 1973.

————. *The Seven Storey Mountain*. New York: Harcourt, Brace, 1948.

Midgley, Mary. *Evolution as a Religion*. Rev. ed. London: Routledge, 2002.

Milton, Richard. *Shattering the Myths of Darwinism*. 2nd ed. Rochester, Vt.: Park Street Press, 1997.

Monroe, Robert A. *Far Journeys*. New York: Broadway, 1985.

————. *Journeys out of the Body*. New York: Broadway, 1971.

————. *Ultimate Journey*. New York: Broadway, 1994.

Müller, Max. *Six Systems of Indian Philosophy*. London: Longmans, Green, 1912.

Nicoll, Maurice. *Living Time and the Integration of the Life*. London: Vincent Stuart, 1952.

Niebuhr, H. Richard. *Christ and Culture*. San Francisco: Harper & Row, 1951.

Niebuhr, Reinhold. *The Nature and Destiny of Man*. 2 vols. Louisville, Ky.: Westminster/John Knox, 1964.

Nikhilananda, Swami. *The Upanishads: A New Translation*. 3rd ed. 4 vols. New York: Ramakrishna-Vivekananda Center, 1990.

Nisargadatta Maharaj. *The Experience of Nothingness*. Edited by Robert Powell. San Diego: Blue Dove, 1996.

Norbu, Namkhai. *Dzogchen: The Self-Perfected State*. Translated by John Shane. Ithaca, N.Y.: Snow Lion, 1996.

Osborne, Arthur, ed. *The Teachings of Bhagavan Sri Ramana Maharshi in His Own Words*. London: Rider, 1962.

Ouspensky, P. D. *In Search of the Miraculous: Fragments of a Forgotten Teaching*. New York: Harcourt, Brace, 1949.

————. *The Psychology of Man's Possible Evolution*. New York: Knopf, 1972.

Penrose, Roger. *The Emperor's New Mind*. Oxford: Oxford University Press, 1989.

Plato. *The Collected Dialogues*. Edited by Edith Hamilton and Huntington Cairns. Princeton: Princeton, NJ../Bollingen, 1961.

———. *Republic*. Translated by Robin Waterfield. Oxford: Oxford University Press, 1993.

Plotinus. *The Enneads*. Translated by Stephen MacKenna. Burdett, N.Y.: Larson, 1992.

Popper, Karl. *Popper Selections*. Edited by David Miller. Princeton, N.J.: Princeton University Press, 1985.

Prem, Krishna. *The Yoga of the Bhagavat Gita*. Shaftesbury, Dorset, U.K.: Element, 1988.

Puharich, Andrija. *Beyond Telepathy*. London: Souvenir, 1974.

Rao, K. B. Ramakrishna. *Theism of Pre-Classical Samkhya*. Prasangara, India: University of Mysore, 1966.

Reymond, Lizelle. *To Live Within*. Portland, Ore.: Rudra Press, 1995.

The Rig Veda. Edited and translated by Wendy Doniger O'Flaherty. London: Penguin, 1981.

Robinson, James M., ed. *The Nag Hammadi Library in English*. 1st ed. San Francisco: Harper & Row, 1977.

Row, T. Subba. *Notes on the Bhagavad Gita*. Point Loma, Calif.: Theosophical University Press, 1934.

Russell, Bertrand. *Our Knowledge of the External World as a Field for Scientific Method in Philosophy*. Rev. ed. London: George Allen & Unwin, 1926.

———. *The Problems of Philosophy*. 1912. Reprint, New York: Barnes & Noble, 2004.

Sankaracharya. *Dakshinamurti Stotra*. Translated by Alladi Mahadeva Shastry. 3rd ed. Madras: Samata, 1978.

Schmidt, Marcia Binder. *The Dzogchen Primer: Embracing the Spiritual Path according to the Great Perfection*. Boston: Shambhala, 2002.

Schopenhauer, Arthur. *The World as Will and Representation*. Translated by E. F. J. Payne. 2 vols. New York: Dover, 1966.

Searle, John R. *Minds, Brains, and Science*. Cambridge, Mass.: Harvard University Press, 1984.

Shankara. *Shankara's Crest-Jewel of Discrimination*. Translated by Swami

Prabhavananda and Christopher Isherwood. Hollywood: Vedanta Press, 1947.

Sharma, Arvind. *Advaita Vedanta: An Introduction*. Delhi: Motilal Banarsidass, 2004.

Sherab, Khenchen Palden, and Khenpo Tsewang Dongyal. *Opening to Our Primordial Nature*. 2nd ed. Ithaca, N.Y.: Snow Lion, 2006.

Smoley, Richard. *Forbidden Faith: The Secret History of Gnosticism*. San Francisco: HarperSanFrancisco, 2006.

———. *Inner Christianity: A Guide to the Esoteric Tradition*. Boston: Shambhala, 2002.

Spong, John Shelby. *Jesus for the Non-Religious*. San Francisco: Harper-SanFrancisco, 2007.

———. *A New Christianity for a New World: Why Traditional Faith Is Dying and How a New Faith Is Being Born*. San Francisco: Harper-SanFrancisco, 2002.

Srinivasachari, P. N. *The Philosophy of Visistadvaita*. Adyar, India: Adyar Library and Research Centre, 1943.

Stewart, Matthew. *The Courtier and the Heretic: Leibniz, Spinoza, and the Fate of God in the Modern World*. New York: Norton, 2006.

Storm, Howard. *My Descent into Death: A Second Chance at Life*. New York: Doubleday, 2005.

Suzuki, D. T. *The Zen Doctrine of No-Mind*. Edited by Christmas Humphreys. 2nd ed. London: Rider, 1969.

Swedenborg, Emanuel. *Heaven and Hell*. Translated by George F. Dole. Rev. ed. West Chester, Pa.: Swedenborg Foundation, 2000.

Taylor, John G. *The Race for Consciousness*. Cambridge, Mass.: MIT Press, 1999.

The Thirteen Principal Upanishads. Rev. ed. Translated by R. E. Hume. London: Oxford University Press, 1931.

Tigunait, Pandit Rajmani. *Seven Systems of Indian Philosophy*. Honesdale, Pa.: Himalayan Institute Press, 1983.

Tillich, Paul. *Dynamics of Faith*. New York: Harper & Row, 1957.

Tolstoy, Lev Nikolayevich. *Anna Karenina*. Translated by Margaret Wettlin. 2 vols. Moscow: Progress, 1978.

Torwesten, Hans. *Vedanta: Heart of Hinduism*. New York: Grove Weidenfeld, 1991.

Weatherhead, Leslie D. *The Christian Agnostic*. London: Stodder & Houghton, 1965.

"Who." *Maha Yoga, or the Upanishadic Lore in the Light of the Teachings of Sri Ramana Maharshi*. 4th ed. Tiruvannamalai, India: Sri Niranjananda Swamy, Sri Ramanasramam, 1950.

Wissler, Clark. *Red Man Reservations*. New York: Collier-Macmillan, 1972.

Woodroffe, John. *Sakti and Sakta: Essays and Addresses*. 6th ed. Madras: Ganesh, 1965.

————. *The Serpent Power*. 7th ed. Madras: Ganesh, 1964.

Yeats, W. B., and Shree Purohit Swami. *The Ten Principal Upanishads*. New York: Macmillan, 1937.

Yogi Publication Society. "Three Initiates." *The Kybalion*. N.p.: Yogi Publication Society, 1908.

Zaehner, R. C., ed. and trans. *The Bhagavad-Gita*. New York: Oxford University Press, 1969.

Zimmer, Heinrich. *Philosophies of India*. Edited by Joseph Campbell. London: Routledge & Kegan Paul, 1952.

PERMISSIONS ACKNOWLEDGMENTS

I gratefully acknowledge the Theosophical Publishing House, Wheaton, Illinois, for permission to use excerpts from Phillip Gowins's *The Sovereign Soul: Sufism, a Path for Today*; Dharma Publishing, Berkeley, California, for permission to use an excerpt from Longchenpa's *Kindly Bent to Ease Us*, vol. 1; and Snow Lion Publications, Ithaca, New York, for permission to use an excerpt from Namkhai Norbu's *Dzogchen: The Self-Perfected State*.

INDEX

The Dice Game of Shiva

attributes
    as belonging to *prakriti*, 51
    of Shiva, 19, 25
Atziluth, 93, 95
Augustine, Saint, 69
authority, 136–38, 162
aversion, 82
avidya (ignorance), 58
Ayer, A. J., 11, 149

B

Babylon, 117–18
Bad Sleep Well, The (Kurosawa), 116–17
being, 33, 95–96
Berkeley, George, 16, 31–32
Bethge, Eberhard, 1–2
Bhagavad Gita, 45, 46, 127
Bible
    on creation, 41, 79
    on faith, 139, 140, 143–45
    on higher reality, 158
    on history of Jews, 117–18
    on Jacob's ladder, 106
    on justice, 118–19, 129
    on knowledge, 175
    on mystical experience, 149
    on sin, 140–41
    on true Self, 152–53
    translations of, 159–60
Binah, 80
Blavatsky H. P., 46, 112, 167
Bogomilism, 42
Bonhoeffer, Dietrich, 1–2, 4–5, 10
Brahman
    all as, 54, 55, 57
    as atman, 39–40, 53, 159
    as experiencer, 56
    without qualities, 85
brain
    consciousness and, 13
    experience of God and, 12, 94
    mind and, 23
    unreal experience and, 94–95
Briah, 93, 95
Brihadaranyaka Upanishad, 131
Buber, Martin, 165
Buddha, 134
Buddha-nature, 131, 153
buddhi (cognition), 79, 80–81, 85

Buddhism
    Four Noble Truths and, 82
    ground of consciousness in, 113
    impersonal absolute in, 129
    liberation and, 105
    no-self in, 130
    power of mind and, 89
    realms of existence in, 95, 103–4
    six *lokas* of, 121
    Theravada and Mahayana, 134
    Three Poisons and, 82
    Tibetan, 29, 89, 153
    vipassana and, 102

C

Cases of the Reincarnation Type (Stevenson), 124
categories
    of Kant, 72, 74, 77, 85, 151
Catharism, 42
Catullus, 172
causality, 31, 72
causation
    characteristics of, 12, 69–70, 84
    constant conjunction and, 66–67, 71, 75, 84
    God/gods in, 63
    gunas and, 83–84
    karmic, 128–29
    limitations of, 101–2
    synchronicity and, 110–11
    types of causes and, 64–65
cave allegory, 74–75, 78
Center for Non-Dualism, 44
change, 165–66
cheating in dice game, 19, 49
chimpanzees, 2–3, 115
Christian Agnostic, The (Weatherhead), 136–37
Christianity
    dualism and, 43–44
    faith in, 136–38
    God and Self as separate in, 154
    God in, 129, 136, 156, 158, 160–61
    justice and, 127
    origins of, 120
    paradox in, 5
    realms of existence and, 103, 104
    reincarnation and, 123–24

204

Urban Rudolf von, 36
Urgrund ("primordial ground"), 85
U.S. elections of 2000, 107–8

V

Vaisheshika, 45
Varieties of Religious Experience (James),
    11
Vedanta
    as Hindu *darshan*, 45
    in modern Indian philosophy, 57–58
    Samkhya and, 46
    See also Advaita Vedanta school
Vedas, 45, 53
via positiva, 57
vibration, 166
vipassana meditation, 102–3
Vivekananda, Swami, 53

W

wakefulness, 34
water, 97
Weatherhead, Leslie D., 136–37
Weizenbaum, Joseph, 171
will
        conscious action and, 92
        as dynamic of *prakriti*, 80
        as eternal, 30–31
        faith as act of, 141–43

"Will to Believe, The" (James), 142
Wissler, Clark, 91
Woodroffe, John, 15, 40
Woolger, Roger, 124
world, 21, 32
World as Will and Representation, The
    (Schopenhauer), 91–92
Worlds of Enlightenment and Retribution,
    104–5, 122
worldview(s)
    Christian, 10
    competing, 173
    scientific, 17, 22, 65–66

X

Xenophanes, 150, 151

Y

Yetzirah (world of forms), 93, 95, 97
Yoga, 45–46
Yogachara school, 113
Yoga Vasistha, 56

Z

Zen practice, 89
Zeus, 84
Zimmer, Heinrich, 45, 53

ABOUT THE AUTHOR

Richard Smoley is one of the world's leading authorities on the mystical and esoteric teachings of Western civilization. He holds a bachelor's degree magna cum laude in classics from Harvard and a BA and MA from the Honour School of Literae Humaniores (classics and philosophy) at The University of Oxford.

Richard served for eight years as editor of *Gnosis: A Journal of the Western Inner Traditions*. He is the author of six books. Currently he is executive editor of *Quest*, the members' journal for the Theosophical Society in America. In addition, he is editor of Quest Books, a publisher of books on spirituality and esotericism operated by the Theosophical Society. His website is www.innerchristianity.com.

NEW WORLD LIBRARY is dedicated to publishing books and other media that inspire and challenge us to improve the quality of our lives and the world.

We are a socially and environmentally aware company, and we strive to embody the ideals presented in our publications. We recognize that we have an ethical responsibility to our customers, our staff members, and our planet.

We serve our customers by creating the finest publications possible on personal growth, creativity, spirituality, wellness, and other areas of emerging importance. We serve New World Library employees with generous benefits, significant profit sharing, and constant encouragement to pursue their most expansive dreams.

As a member of the Green Press Initiative, we print an increasing number of books with soy-based ink on 100 percent postconsumer-waste recycled paper. Also, we power our offices with solar energy and contribute to nonprofit organizations working to make the world a better place for us all.

Our products are available
in bookstores everywhere.
For our catalog, please contact:

New World Library
14 Pamaron Way
Novato, California 94949

Phone: 415-884-2100 or 800-972-6657
Catalog requests: Ext. 50
Orders: Ext. 52
Fax: 415-884-2199
Email: escort@newworldlibrary.com

To subscribe to our electronic newsletter, visit
www.newworldlibrary.com

HELPING TO PRESERVE OUR ENVIRONMENT

New World Library uses 100% postconsumer-waste recycled paper for our books whenever possible, even if it costs more. During 2008 this choice saved the following precious resources:

46,104
trees were saved

www.newworldlibrary.com

ENERGY	WASTEWATER	GREENHOUSE GASES	SOLID WASTE
32 MILLION BTU	17 MILLION GAL.	4 MILLION LB.	2 MILLION LB.

Environmental impact estimates were made using the Environmental Defense Fund Paper Calculator @ www.papercalculator.org.